Praise for *One Lord, On*

"With his usual fire and enthusiasm, Jesse Romero and his co-writer, Paul Zucarelli, have given us a gem of a book that will affirm and strengthen the faith of those already Catholic and provide a light to the path of those seeking to understand. And if arguments loom up against the one true Church, this book will answer them in a gentle, convincing manner. This book makes a good read, a good gift, and a good means to share the truth with non-Catholics."

— ***Steve Ray,*** catholicconvert.com

"Since the 1980s, I have had the privilege of knowing and working in the vineyard alongside many fellow Catholics who have poured their lives into the mission of explaining, defending, and sharing the biblical truth of Jesus Christ and the Catholic Church He founded. Jesse Romero stands as a champion among them in terms of the sheer passion, expansiveness, and bang-on-the-bull's-eye certainty he brings to the task. *One Lord, One Faith, One Church* is a tour de force combination of all those gifts."

— ***Patrick Madrid,*** host of the daily *Patrick Madrid Show* on Relevant Radio

"I'm pleased to add my voice to support for this important work. Criticism of the Roman Catholic Church has always been easy because of her human flaws, but is she something more? Does she truly have a divine origin? Was she actually begun by Jesus Christ, God's Divine Son? Is she guided by the Holy Spirit today to seek ever deeper holiness? Saints and martyrs through twenty centuries have known the answers to these questions, and you will find them in these pages as well. Join us in the adventure."

— ***Bishop Joseph E. Strickland,*** Bishop of the Diocese of Tyler, Texas

ONE LORD, ONE FAITH, ONE CHURCH

Jesse Romero & Paul Zucarelli

ONE LORD, ONE FAITH, ONE CHURCH
— *An Inconvenient Truth* —

SOPHIA INSTITUTE PRESS
Manchester, New Hampshire

Copyright © 2024 by Zucarelli Family Faith Charitable Trust and Jesse Romero.
Printed in the United States of America. All rights reserved.

Cover by Emma Helstrom

Cover image: Jesus Christ statue by Arturo Rey (Unsplash Vk7GGQCg); Facade of St. John Lateran's Basilica by Marek Poplawski (ShutterStock 1731655297)

Unless otherwise noted, biblical references in this book are taken from the Catholic Edition of the Revised Standard Version of the Bible, copyright 1965, 1966 by the Division of Christian Education of the National Council of the Churches of Christ in the United States of America. Used by permission. All rights reserved.

Excerpts from the English translation of the *Catechism of the Catholic Church* for use in the United States of America copyright © 1994, United States Catholic Conference, Inc. — Libreria Editrice Vaticana. English translation of the *Catechism of the Catholic Church: Modifications from the Editio Typica* copyright © 1997, United States Conference of Catholic Bishops — Libreria Editrice Vaticana.

No part of this book may be reproduced, stored in a retrieval system, or transmitted in any form, or by any means, electronic, mechanical, photocopying, or otherwise, without the prior written permission of the publisher, except by a reviewer, who may quote brief passages in a review.

Sophia Institute Press
Box 5284, Manchester, NH 03108
1-800-888-9544
www.SophiaInstitute.com

Sophia Institute Press is a registered trademark of Sophia Institute.

paperback ISBN 979-8-88911-320-1

ebook ISBN 979-8-88911-321-8

Library of Congress Control Number: 2024937872

Second printing

Dedication

This book is dedicated to Jesus Christ. It is written out of our love for our triune God, in whom we live and move and have our being. It is our hope to share, with our neighbors, the fullness of Truth that is found in Christ Jesus. We pray that the evidence we will present will resonate with your heart, and that God will lead you to a deeper conversion in the Name of Jesus the Lord.

We also pray to God our Father that the Romero and Zucarelli families, and our descendants, may be blessed with abundant grace and mercy.

We ask this through Jesus Christ, Our Lord. Amen.

Contents

Introduction. 3
1. Divine Origin Is Necessary 5
2. Christendom A.D. 33 to A.D. 1517 21
3. Religious Revolution in Europe: The Triggering Event 41
4. The Reformation Spreads to the Americas 71
5. Defining the Term *Church* in the United States of America 99
6. The Church as the Living Bride of Christ 123
7. Intelligent Dissent: The Cause of Disunity 145
8. Do You Need Evidentiary Supernatural Proof? 165
9. Unity and Continuity Do Matter to God 189
10. Words of Encouragement 207
Epilogue. 217
About the Authors 219

One Lord, One Faith, One Church

Introduction

NONE OF US KNOW the hour when we shall pass from this earth and meet God. But it is certain that we will. If you are unsure about that, perhaps this book will help lead you to faith, and to understand how faith in Jesus Christ has allowed countless millions to face the unknown future with confidence.

People with faith intuitively know the future for every human being: death, judgment, Heaven, or Hell. This book will explore these ultimate realities in an open and honest dialogue to provoke critical thinking. It will present facts in human history that are irrefutable, and pose questions and present answers that are relevant, comprehensive, detailed, and factually based.

Readers need not have theological training nor any advanced religious academic studies to read this book. Specifically, it was written because so many people within the last three to four generations were never taught about their faith, and if they learned anything, it was often incorrect — particularly about other people's faith. We will bring readers to the Nexus of Truth: Jesus Christ. We will systemically link persons and events and show their causality. By learning the history of Christianity, readers will be able to understand how it came to be. God willing, they will come to see that the God-Man, Jesus, is Himself the link between mankind and eternal life.

But if Jesus is the answer to our questions, why are there so many churches? How did they come into existence? Why do they profess and teach such different things about Jesus, particularly things that are very different regarding our salvation? Why do so many churches have no written, or even fixed, doctrine? How can one discern the Truth among so many diverse belief systems, all of which claim to profess the Truth in Jesus Christ? This book will address these questions comprehensively and factually. Since Jesus is the narrow gate, it is imperative that we enter only through His Mystical Body.

It all comes back to the connection between God and mankind. Since our Divine God came amongst humanity in the form of Jesus, what He said and did must take precedence over anything that mere mortals say about Him. Jesus is the Nexus between God and man. So we will utilize the Bible and focus on Jesus, the Word made flesh: "And the Word became flesh and dwelt among us, full of grace and truth; we have beheld his glory, glory as of the only Son from the Father" (John 1:14).

We pray that you read, contemplate, study, verify, and prayerfully discern if Jesus or God the Father started thousands of churches. To aid your discernment, we will help you address thematic questions, such as: Can Jesus Christ Himself be the foundation of just any "church"? Did God intend to create an unlimited number of churches with differing beliefs and practices? What is a *church* and how does God define the word *church* versus how man defines it? How did we get to having so many varying churches?

Finally, we will ask: Did God the Father and Jesus Christ His Son truly start the Roman Catholic Church?

Regardless of where you are in your walk with the Lord and your personal faith journey, we pray this book leads you to the fullness of Truth: Jesus Christ Himself.

CHAPTER 1

Divine Origin Is Necessary

If you love me, you will keep my commandments. (John 14:15)

We must start with a basic truth: divine revelation, revealed in the Bible by God Himself, is paramount to our Faith. At the Last Supper, Jesus could not have been more direct. If we love Him, we will keep His commandments. We should follow Our Lord's instruction.

Jesus was not telling the disciples that following the Ten Commandments alone would show their love for Him. He didn't reveal true "love" for Him as only the Ten Commandments or the laws for the people of Israel — for He fulfilled the Law. Rather, He gave us an if-then proposition: "*If* you love me, [*then*] you *will* keep [*all*] my commandments" (John 14:15; all emphases added).

Of course, this love would include obeying the Ten Commandments. But it also would include all his teachings, preaching, Beatitudes, exhortations, and explanations of His parables. All these combined represent His commandments to humanity. However, since we are all human creatures, we think we can figure this God "thing" out all by ourselves. To be properly ordered in our rational thinking, we must begin with God Himself. What He says matters.

God gave each of us not only our existence but also our intellect and free will. In the natural world, we have five senses: sight, smell, taste, touch, and sound. It is how we process all information into our finite intellect. But remember: our intellect is truly finite. Therefore, not only do we use our sense of sound to hear but we also use it to communicate our thoughts to others with words (sounds). It is our words that give meaning to people and only through words can we communicate what we think and feel.

God uses words too. In fact, He is "the Word." The Word is a Person, Jesus Christ. He is an eternal Person, just like us, but begotten not made, without sin, and seated on the throne at the right hand of God the Father. He will come to judge the living and the dead.

Who Is Jesus?

Let us again revisit the Gospel of John which eloquently describes who God is and why Jesus as the second Person of the Holy Trinity **preexisted human time and space**. Let us also consider the equally important question: Why did God send us His only Son? The Bible recounts:

> In the beginning was the Word [Jesus], and the Word [Jesus] was with God, and the Word [Jesus] was God. **He [Jesus] was in the beginning with God**; all things were made through him, and without him was not anything made that was made." (John 1:1–3; emphasis added)

> And again: "**And the *Word* became flesh and dwelt among us**, full of grace and truth; we have beheld his glory, glory as of the only Son from the Father. (John bore witness to him, and cried, 'This was he of whom I said, "He who comes after me ranks before me, **because he**

> [Jesus] was before me."' And from his fulness have we all received, grace upon grace. For the law was given through Moses; **grace and *truth* came through Jesus Christ. No one has ever seen God; the only Son, who is in the bosom of the Father, he has made him known.** (John 1:14–18; all emphases added)

In the book of Revelation, when Jesus returns, John gives Jesus three names using, again, words to communicate to us the meaning of who Jesus is. He states, "He is clad in a robe dipped in blood, and the **name by which he [Jesus] is called is The Word of God**" (Rev. 19:13; emphasis added). John also names Jesus "Faithful and True" and "King of kings and Lord of lords" as the other names within the same chapter of the book of Revelation (Rev. 19:11, 16).

What Did Jesus Say about the Church?

If God became man in Christ Jesus, and if Jesus is the Word, then it is essential to listen to what He says and commands us in His own words. Let us study this question together.

Let us look at the word *church* in Sacred Scripture. First, there is no use of the word *church* in the Old Testament. Rather, the Hebrew word in the Old Testament is *qahal*, which translates to "congregation" or "assembly of believers." It is a reference to the synagogues. However, the word *church* does appear in the New Testament quite often. The first time that this word appears in the New Testament is when Jesus responds to Peter's statement, or confession, of who Jesus is:

> He [Jesus] said to them, "But who do you say that I am?" Simon Peter replied, "You are the Christ, the Son of the living God." And Jesus answered him, "Blessed are you, Simon Bar-Jona! For flesh and blood has not revealed this

to you, but my Father who is in heaven. And I tell you, **you are Peter, and on this rock I will build *my church* [*ekklesia*]**, and the powers of death shall not prevail against it. **I will give *you* the keys to the *kingdom of heaven*, and whatever *you* bind on earth shall be bound in heaven, and whatever *you* loose on earth shall be loosed in heaven.**" (Matt. 16:15–19; all emphases added)

Let us note the following: God the Father gave divine revelation to Peter, not Jesus, the second Person of the Trinity. Jesus Himself testifies to this fact in Matthew 16:17 by responding, "Blessed are you, Simon Bar-Jona! For flesh and blood has not revealed this to you, but **my Father who is in heaven**" (emphasis added).

Once this occurs, and Simon Peter speaks the revelation, Jesus establishes His Church upon Him. He even gives him the keys to the Kingdom of Heaven. This is more than symbolic. Just as God chose Eliakim to be the ultimate keyholder or gatekeeper able to grant access to the house of David at his discretion, Peter alone has the authority and power from God to open and shut. (In Luke 3:30, Jesus is listed as a descendant from Eliakim, who was the keyholder in the Old Testament for God's Chosen.)

Now that the Word was dwelling with us, God chose Peter and simultaneously Jesus gave him the authority over His Church. The Bible is clear: not only did God choose Peter, but Jesus renamed him *Petros* or *Petra* in the Greek, meaning "Rock." Furthermore, Peter is known by the corresponding Aramaic word *Kepha* or *Cephas*. The meaning of these is also "Rock." Jesus made Peter the leader of His Church on earth. At no other time in human history did God Himself state that He was going to start a Church upon a man and then give him authority and the keys to the Kingdom of Heaven. This is the divine origin of the Church.

Immediately after Peter (through God's revelation) declares Jesus to be the Messiah, Jesus takes Peter, James, and John to Mount Tabor for His Transfiguration. Note that this happens on the seventh day after Christ establishes His Church upon Peter. The number seven confers God's completeness and perfection. Remember how Peter declared Jesus the Christ? Jesus will now prove it to him along with two witnesses, James, and John. In addition to living human beings witnessing the glorified Jesus, two other pairs of persons bear witness to Jesus being God. The first pair is Moses and Elijah, men themselves representing all historical prophets and the Law. Additionally, God the Father (the first Person of the Holy Trinity) along with the Holy Spirit (the third Person of the Holy Trinity) bear witness that Jesus is the second Person of the Trinity — the Christ. So, there are three sets of two witnesses who establish the fact that Jesus truly is who Peter says He is. All facts and the truth and validity of someone's claim must be established based on two or three witnesses (Matt. 18:16–18).

After this event in human history, Jesus gave the same authority that the Father gave to Peter to the remaining apostles in Matthew 18. He also told the apostles exactly what God had said in Deuteronomy — that every fact must be verified by two or three witnesses (Deut. 19:15). All the apostles were given the authority to bind and loose on earth and in Heaven. This is the second time the word *church* appears in the New Testament:

> Every word may be confirmed by the evidence of two or three witnesses. If he refuses to listen to them, tell it to the **church**; and if he refuses **to listen even to the church**, let him be to you as a Gentile and a tax collector. Truly, I say to **you [the apostles], whatever you bind on earth shall be**

bound in heaven, and whatever you loose on earth shall be loosed in heaven. (Matt. 18:16–18; all emphases added)

Why Is the Church in Rome?

But why would Christianity's headquarters move from Jerusalem to Rome? Didn't Jesus pick the twelve apostles in the Holy Land and establish His Church there? Yes, this is where she started. But Jesus Himself said that Jerusalem would be destroyed within the current generation and that not one stone would remain of the Temple — which ended up occurring in A.D. 70. God used the pagan Roman Empire to accomplish this brutality, which God had actually prophesied through Jeremiah the prophet:

> But my people have forgotten me,
> they burn incense to false gods;
> they have stumbled in their ways,
> in the ancient roads,
> and have gone into bypaths,
> not the highway,
> making their land a horror,
> a thing to be hissed at forever.
> Everyone who passes by it is horrified
> and shakes his head.
> Like the east wind I will scatter them
> before the enemy.
> I will show them my back, not my face,
> in the day of their calamity. (Jer. 18:15–17)

But why would God choose Rome to be the headquarters on earth for Christianity? God knows what He is doing. Have you heard the saying, "All roads lead to Rome"? They did. The Roman Empire designed roads to quickly transport cattle, materials, and armies to support the empire. This hub and spoke configuration meant that all roads did lead to Rome. In fact, this was perhaps the pagan empire's greatest achievement.

The Roman Empire's roads spanned more than four hundred thousand kilometers, including over eighty thousand kilometers that were paved. The Romans moved armies, traded goods, and communicated news to the world. At the height of its power, no fewer than twenty-nine military highways radiated from Rome. There were 113 Roman provinces connected by 372 great road links. The Roman Empire also perfected water canals to ensure that population growth continued for the empire. Once Rome was converted, God would harness the political power of Rome to bring about a great evangelization and conversion of all peoples in the world. First, the European continent (St. James — Spain ca. A.D. 40), then the New World of North and South America (Columbus in 1492 and Our Lady of Guadalupe in 1531), to the ends of the world today.

Now, one might ask: Where is Rome mentioned in the Bible? Rome is mentioned fifteen times in the New Testament and thirteen times in the Old Testament. Rome is relevant to God's plan for salvation history. Let us examine why this is such an important issue for the Church and ourselves.

The Importance of Peter

Peter was a native of Bethsaida, a village near Lake Tiberius. Peter was the son of John. His name was Simon and he lived and worked as a fisherman on Lake Gennesaret, or as we know it, the Sea of Galilee. His brother Andrew introduced him to Jesus, who gave him the name *Cephas*, the Aramaic equivalent of the Greek name *Peter* ("the Rock"). He was present at Jesus' first miracle at the wedding at Cana and his own home in Capernaum when Jesus cured his mother-in-law. When Our Lord hears Simon publicly acknowledge that He is "The Christ ... the Son of the living God," Jesus declares that He will build His Church upon him.

Jesus also says that Peter will possess the keys of Heaven, as mentioned earlier. Peter also has the authority to bind and loose on earth and in Heaven, which is outside of the human dimensions of time and space (Matt. 16:15–19).

These statements are the scriptural foundation for the Catholic teaching that Peter was the first pope and for the Catholic belief in the primacy of Peter and its origin from Christ. Peter is mentioned more frequently in the Bible than all other apostles — 193 times when reviewing the names Peter, Simon Peter, Simon, or Cephas. Peter's name is listed first when Scripture lists the apostles (Matt. 10:1–4; Mark 3:15–19; Luke 6:13–16; Acts 1:13). Other examples from Sacred Scripture that demonstrably present Peter as the leader of the Church include but are not limited to:

1. Peter was spoken of directly by Jesus as the preeminent shepherd of Christ's flock. This was done by the resurrected or glorified Jesus Himself (John 21:15–17). He was given this responsibility by Jesus over the universal Church, which Jesus founded upon Peter before His Resurrection. Other apostles had similar but subordinate responsibilities (Acts 20:28; 1 Pet. 5:2).

2. Even the Jewish leaders regarded Peter as the spokesperson for Christianity and their leader of the Church (Acts 4:1–13). The common people of Jesus' time also recognized Peter as the leader of the Church (Acts 2:37–41; 5:15).

3. Peter was specifically designated by an angel of God to testify to the Resurrection (Mark 16:7).

4. Peter was the first person to speak after the Pentecost event and the first Christian to preach the gospel (Acts 2:14–36).

5. Peter was the first to perform a miracle himself in Acts 3:6–12, and he was the only apostle to bring an anathema upon a self-professed member of the Church as confirmed by God Himself (God's judgment of death upon Ananias and Sapphira in Acts 5:2–11).

6. An angel told Cornelius the centurion to seek out only Peter for instruction and guidance in Christianity (Acts 10:1–6). Peter thus was the first to receive the Gentiles for conversion to the Church after divine revelation (Acts 10:9–48).

7. Peter was the first of the apostles (and one of only two) who raised the dead by the power of the Holy Spirit dwelling in him (Acts 9:40).

8. Peter was the first to preach repentance and the requirement of Baptism. Also, Peter commanded that Gentile Christians be baptized (Acts 2:38; 10:44–48).

9. In Paul's own words and at the beginning of his missionary work, Paul specifically visited Jerusalem to see Peter for fifteen days (Gal. 1:18). Paul voluntarily visited with Peter, James and John to ensure that he was preaching "the faith which was once for all delivered to the saints" (Jude 3).

10. According to biblical scholars, Peter wrote his first epistle from Rome as Bishop of Rome. He was the leader and spokesperson for the Church. In 1 Peter 5:13, he said, "She who is at Babylon, who is likewise chosen, sends you greetings; and so does my son Mark." *Babylon* was the code word used for Rome, as anyone who spoke ill of the empire was often killed. Paul confirmed in his epistle to the Roman Church that someone other than himself established the Church in Rome before he wanted to visit there. In Romans 15:20 he said, "Thus [I make] it my ambition to preach the gospel, **not where Christ has already been named,** *lest* **I build upon another man's foundation**" (emphasis added). Peter had already established the Church in Rome.

These are only a few of the Bible verses that depict that Christ chose Peter as God chose Noah, Abraham, Isaac, Jacob, Moses, and David as leaders of His salvific plan for humanity.

Peter Was in Rome

Peter would end up in Rome, martyred in the city of the church that he established. He was crucified upside down at the foot of Vatican Hill during the reign of Emperor Nero. Peter's body lies in a tomb underneath the altar at St. Peter's Basilica in Rome. Corroboration of the aforementioned is the writing of Eusebius of Caesarea. Eusebius was the bishop of Caesarea Maritima in the Roman province of Syria Palaestina. He was regarded as one of the most learned Christians during late antiquity and a scholar of the biblical canon. As a Church historian, he wrote: "In the second year of the two hundredth and fifth Olympiad [A.D. 42]: The Apostle Peter, after he established the

Church in Antioch, is sent to **Rome, where he remains as bishop of that city, preaching the gospel for twenty-five years.**"[1]

Why did the Church have to get to Rome? Because Jesus Himself prophesied that Jerusalem and the Temple therein would be destroyed within the current generation while He walked the earth. This is recorded in Matthew 24:1–2. In A.D. 70, the Romans destroyed Jerusalem, slaughtered virtually everyone, and destroyed the Temple.

One might ask: Did Jesus tell the apostles and the Church to leave Jerusalem? The answer is a resounding yes. At the Great Commission, Our Lord told all the apostles to leave Jerusalem because the generation of the Jews that rejected their Messiah had now triggered a divine chastisement.

Old Testament Prophecies about the Church Being in Rome

Does the Old Testament prophesy that the Kingdom of the Messiah will be headquartered in Rome? Yes. The book of Daniel illuminates three themes: 1) the sovereignty of God; 2) the self-destructive pride of mankind; and 3) the ultimate victory of God's Kingdom. Daniel was a great prophet who rose during the Babylonian exile. He defied many attempts by Babylonian rulers to worship their pagan gods. In his visions, he foresaw the end of King Nebuchadnezzar's kingdom. Daniel prophesied that four kingdoms would enslave Judah and that the Jews and Jesus would establish God's Kingdom, which is His Church, in Rome by crushing pagan Rome. The rise and fall of human empires were prophesied by Daniel.

In chapter 2 of the book of Daniel, Nebuchadnezzar, King of Babylon, had a dream that described the succession of world empires. In his dream, he saw a great image of a head of gold, a chest

---

[1] William A. Jurgens, *The Faith of the Early Fathers* vol. I (Collegeville: Liturgical Press, 1970), p. 291.

and arms of silver, a belly and thighs of brass, and legs of iron and feet partly of iron and partly of clay. Then he saw a **stone cut without human hands which came down from Heaven and destroyed the entire image** (Dan. 2:31–35).

Babylon Prophesied

The head of gold represents the king of the kingdom of Babylon which God gave to Nebuchadnezzar to rule (Dan. 2:36–38). Babylon ruled as the world power from 605 B.C. to 539 B.C. The silver breast and arms and the brass belly and thighs of the image represent other nations that would arise after Babylon falls (Dan. 2:39).

Medo-Persia Prophesied

Daniel 5:22–31 describes the fall of the Babylonian Empire to the Medes and Persians. The Medes and Persians defeated the Babylonians in 539 B.C. They would remain the new world power until 332 B.C. The Medes and the Persians are represented by the silver breast and arms.

Greece Prophesied

Twice in the book of Daniel we are told that the Medes and the Persians would be defeated by the Greeks (Dan. 8:4–7, 20–21; 11:1–3). The Greeks defeated the Medes and the Persians in 331 B.C. and are represented by the brass belly and thighs of the image. The kingdom of Greece would rule over the whole world under Alexander the Great. After his death it would be divided into four kingdoms until 168 B.C. (Dan. 2:39–40).

Rome Prophesied

The iron legs and feet of iron and clay represent the fourth world empire — **Rome** (Dan. 2:40). Rome defeated the Greeks in 168 B.C. Rome is well-described in the Bible as an empire that crushes like iron. It will break and smash things, but its partial clay feet depict that the empire is somehow divided. It is both strong and brittle. Rome crucified six hundred Greek slave soldiers from Sparta along the Appian Way to show the other nations what happens to the enemies of Rome.

Christ's Kingdom — The Catholic Church

In the end, **the stone cut without human hands would come down from Heaven and destroy** the human kingdoms. Christ's Kingdom will crush all earthly kingdoms (Dan. 2:34–35, 41–45). This stone that was not cut out of human hands struck the statue and destroyed it. This stone became a great mountain and filled the whole earth (Dan. 2:44–45). It is the Messiah who is prophesied as the **great stone** who will crush all the kingdoms of the world, become a great mountain, and fill the earth. This everlasting Kingdom is Our Lord Jesus Christ and His Body, the Church — the stone that crushes earthly kingdoms. As St. Peter states in 1 Peter 2:4–8:

> Come to him, to that **living stone**, rejected by men but in God's sight chosen and precious; and like **living stones** be yourselves built into a spiritual house [the Church], to be a holy priesthood, to offer spiritual sacrifices acceptable to God through Jesus Christ. For it stands in scripture: "Behold, I am laying in Zion a stone, a cornerstone chosen and precious, and he who believes in him will not be put to shame." To you therefore who believe, he is precious, but for those who do not believe, "The very stone which the builders rejected has become the head of the corner," and "A stone that will make men stumble, a rock that will make them fall"; for they stumble because they disobey the word, as they were destined to do. (all emphases added)

What Daniel teaches us is that man will never build an everlasting empire nor one that will usher in a millennium of peace. Only God's Kingdom will reign forever. These four kingdoms described via this great image precede the Messiah, who will oppose all pagan kingdoms. These pagan kingdoms are personifications of Satan. Daniel drives this point home in chapter 7. Here we see that all the earthly kingdoms are temporary and fleeting no matter how impressive their militaries appear to be. Ultimately, the Son of Man — Jesus Himself — will usher in the Eternal Kingdom of God the Father, who is called "the Ancient of Days" (Dan. 7:13–16, 17–18, 27).

God will cause the empire of Rome to fall too, and then Christianity's headquarters will be established in Rome along with its mission to proclaim the gospel to the entire world. Rome was strategically chosen by the Lord to carry out **His** universal mission of salvation for humanity. That is why the Scriptures say, "These men [the apostles] have turned the world upside down" (Acts 17:6).

Why Did Jesus Pick Twelve to Govern His Church?

We will end this chapter of human history with another question: Why did Jesus pick twelve to govern His Church? The number twelve represents God's perfection and authority. It is often used to display the governing structure that God establishes on earth and in Heaven. That is why there are twelve minor Old Testament prophets, Jacob has twelve sons who will become the twelve tribes of Israel, and, of course, twelve apostles. In chapter 21 of the book of the Apocalypse, the New Jerusalem, or the Kingdom of Heaven, has twelve gates with the names of the twelve tribes of Israel and twelve angels guarding each gate. It also has twelve foundations with the names of the twelve apostles. It is no accident that God chose twelve men to form Israel. God's Chosen People, the Israelites, were divided by God into twelve tribes. When Jesus arrived on earth,

He called out twelve men to form a new people for Himself. The Church is the new Israel. From the beginning of all time, God created and chose the twelve apostles to start his Church knowing that Judas was a devil. "Jesus answered them, 'Did I not choose you, the twelve, and one of you is a devil?'" (John 6:70).

Jesus spoke plainly about Judas Iscariot, for He knew that one of the twelve was to betray Him. In the Gospel of Mark 3:13–19, it states: "And he went up into the hills, and **called to him those whom he desired**; and they came to him. And he appointed twelve, to be with him, and to be sent out to preach and have authority to cast out demons: Simon whom he surnamed Peter; James the son of Zebedee and John the brother of James, whom he surnamed Boanerges, that is, sons of thunder; Andrew, and Philip, and Bartholomew, and Matthew, and Thomas, and James the son of Alphaeus, and Thaddaeus, and Simon the Cananaean, and Judas Iscariot, **who betrayed him**" (all emphases added).

Remember that Jesus Christ, our **King**, built a **Kingdom** which is His **Church** (His Body), and that He left **Peter** in charge of His **Kingdom** (until He comes again). His Kingdom is truly upon us: "Thy kingdom come, thy will be done, **on earth as it is in heaven**" (Matt. 6:10; emphasis added).

REFLECTIONS

1. Why was divine revelation given to Simon?

2. Why did Jesus give the chosen Twelve authority?

3. Why is Rome specifically mentioned so often in the Bible?

4. Did Christ personally select the Twelve to build His Church on earth?

CHAPTER 2

CHRISTENDOM A.D. 33 TO A.D. 1517

*You may know how one ought to behave in the household of God, which is **the church of the living God**, the pillar and bulwark **of the truth**. (1 Tim. 3:15; all emphases added)*

IN THE PREVIOUS CHAPTER, we saw where the word *church* was spoken by Our Lord in the context of Jesus building His Church upon the man, Peter, whom He chose, and that the gates of Hell would not prevail against it (Matt. 16:18). The original word for *church* used in sacred text was *ekklesia*. It comes from the Greek word *kaleo* (to call) with the prefix *ek-* (out). Hence, the word means "the called-out ones"; however, the English word *church* in English translations of the Bible does not derive from *ekklesia*, but rather from the word *kuriakon*, and it means "dedicated to the Lord."

This is very important as we begin to address the question: Is Jesus' Church built upon the apostles and their teaching as they were truly called out by Jesus? Or is any church sufficient if a person believes that they are dedicated to the Lord in their personal beliefs, which may or may not be in accord with apostolic teachings?

As we have previously mentioned, the second time the word *ekklesia*, or *church*, appears in the New Testament is in Matthew 18:15–18, when the Lord says, "If your brother sins against you, go and tell him his fault, between you and him alone. If he listens to you, you have gained your brother. But if he does not listen, take one or two others along with you, that every word may be confirmed by the evidence of two or three witnesses. If he refuses to listen to them, **tell it to the *church*; and if he refuses to listen even to the *church*,** let him be to you as a Gentile and a tax collector. Truly, I say to **you** [the apostles — the ones called out], whatever you bind on earth shall be bound in heaven, and whatever you loose on earth shall be loosed in heaven" (all emphases added).

Christ's Body, the Church, grew despite facing many external obstacles and heresies from within. Nonetheless, she began as a very small seed, nourished by the grace of God. We will look at how Rome continued to play its key part in God's salvation history for mankind. Jesus had now died, risen as the firstfruits of the dead, and poured out the Holy Spirit upon many at Pentecost (as the Lord promised). So, let's continue with the early Church and discover how "All Roads Lead to Rome" is a part of God's plan in Christ.

In Acts 2:1–11, the Bible records what happened on the day of Pentecost, and it references all the different ethnic races present and where they are from. In verse 10, Luke states, "**and visitors from Rome**" (emphasis added) — which again shows the importance of Rome to the Church. Then **Peter**, as the appointed leader of the Church, addresses the crowd and explains God's plan of salvation through the Messiah — which again shows that Peter, the itinerant fisherman, was the leader and spokesman of the Church.

Importance of St. Paul

Now, let's look at the greatest missionary for the Church: St. Paul. Why would Jesus choose such a man? He was the antithesis of what one would expect. Saul was a Pharisee whose entire life ambition and goal had been to destroy the Church before she could even get started. (Incidentally, Saul was not renamed by Our Lord like Peter or Abraham. People simply referred to him as Paul after his conversion, as he was the apostle to the Gentiles. (*Paul* is Greek for the name *Saul*, which is Hebrew.)

The embryonic roots of the Church were under attack by Saul, a Pharisee who did not believe that the Messiah had come. But Paul himself would end up in **Rome**, by divine providence.

Let's look at all the Rome references associated with Paul using facts and Scripture.

St. Paul was a Jewish Pharisee and a Roman citizen. He was a Greek-speaking Jew. His father, Antipater, was a Roman citizen, and his mother, Cypros, was a Jew. He was trained and mentored in Judaism by Gamaliel in Jerusalem. Gamaliel was the grandson of Hillel the Elder, a great Jewish leader and rabbi. Gamaliel received the title *Rabban* or "our master," which is considered a rabbi teacher of the highest esteem. This rabbi would play an important role in sparing Peter and the apostles' lives in chapter 5 of the book of Acts, in addition to training Paul in Judaism. Ecclesiastical traditions suggest that Gamaliel secretly supported the early Christians. Photius, a notable scholar, wrote that Gamaliel was baptized by Peter and John, together with his son and Nicodemus.

St. Paul played a critical role in the growth and continuity of Jesus' Church, for which He handpicks the man. Practically speaking, if Christianity needed to be preached and spread in a pagan, Greek-speaking world under pagan Roman rule, then God needed a Greek-speaking Roman citizen who was highly educated under the Mosaic Law and a Jew of high regard. St. Paul was all three, a triple threat to a violent pagan world. Evidently, his selection by Jesus Himself is so important that his personal conversion story is told three times by St. Luke. (The words *church* and *Rome* will appear more often in the book of Acts.)

As St. Paul was persecuting Jesus' Church, Jesus Himself put a stop to it: he blinded Paul, healed him, converted him, and assigned him a life of suffering for Christ Himself to build His Body, which is His Church. Paul was healed and received the Holy Spirit via the laying on of hands by Ananias, the bishop of Damascus. He is baptized by this same bishop.

The Connection of St. Peter and St. Paul to Rome

Let's look at the connection of St. Paul and St. Peter to the City of **Rome** and then study the *ekklesia* (or word for *church*) appearing in the book of Acts. We pray that you discern and understand the connections.

God made Paul Roman because God would send him to Rome. Notice all the Roman references spoken by the Holy Spirit, or the Lord Himself, to Paul.

Acts 16:37–39 records, "But Paul said to them, 'They have beaten us publicly, uncondemned, men who are **Roman citizens**, and have thrown us into prison; and do they now cast us out secretly? No! let them come themselves and take us out.' The police reported these words to the magistrates, and they were afraid when they heard that they were **Roman citizens**; so they came and apologized to them" (all emphases added). God's permissive will allowed Paul, along with Silas, to be arrested and beaten with rods. Eventually, it would be the fact that he was **Roman** that ultimately allowed him to appeal his case to **Rome**.

Acts 19:21 records, "Now after these events Paul resolved in the Spirit to pass through Macedonia and Achaia and go to Jerusalem, saying, 'After I have been there, I must also **see Rome**'" (emphasis added). The Holy Spirit prompted Paul to journey to **Rome**.

Acts 22:17–21 records, "When I had returned to Jerusalem and was praying in the temple, I fell into a trance and saw him [Jesus] saying to me 'Make haste and get quickly out of Jerusalem, because they will not accept your testimony about me.' And I said, 'Lord, they themselves know that in every synagogue I imprisoned and beat those who believed in thee. And when the blood of Stephen thy witness was shed, I also was standing by and approving, and keeping the garments of those who killed him.' And he said to me, 'Depart; for I will send you far away to the Gentiles.'" Paul must get to **Rome**. It is his destiny:

> The tribune commanded him to be brought into the barracks, and ordered him to be examined by scourging, to find out why they shouted thus against him. But when they had tied him up with the thongs, Paul said to the centurion who was standing by, "Is it lawful for you to scourge a man who is a **Roman** citizen, and uncondemned?" When the centurion heard that, he went to the tribune and said to him, "What are you about to do? For this man is a **Roman** citizen." So the tribune came and said to him, "Tell me, are you a **Roman** citizen?" And he said, "Yes." The tribune answered, "I bought this citizenship for a large sum." Paul said, "But I was born a [**Roman**] citizen"; So those who were about to examine him withdrew from him instantly; and the tribune also was afraid, for he realized that Paul was a **Roman** citizen and that he had bound him. (Acts 22:24–29; all emphases added)

Paul's Roman citizenship and birthright is the central fact that gives the Roman guard pause as the Jews plot to kill this man of God. As Jesus was destined to die in the Holy City of Jerusalem, Paul and Peter are destined to die in Rome.

Acts 23:11 records, "The following night the Lord stood by him [Paul] and said, 'Take courage, for as you have testified about me at Jerusalem, so you must bear witness also at **Rome**'" (emphasis added). This verse of Scripture makes it clear that the Lord Himself wanted to use the most eloquent, highly educated apostle to evangelize the Gentiles in Rome and grow the Church that Peter initially established.

Acts 23:27 records, "This man was seized by the Jews, and was about to be killed by them, when I came upon them with soldiers and rescued him, having learned that he was a **Roman** citizen (emphasis added). Notice how God saved Paul many times because He needed him to carry out His mission to evangelize in **Rome**.

In Acts 25 through 28, Paul, as a **Roman** citizen, appeals to Caesar because he knows that the Jews wish to kill him. This ensures that he ends up in **Rome**.

Once in **Rome**, St. Paul's life ends preaching there:

> There we found brethren, and were invited to stay with them for seven days. And so we came to **Rome**.... And when we came into **Rome,** Paul was allowed to stay by himself, with the soldier that guarded him. After three days he called together the local leaders of the Jews; and when they had gathered, he said to them, "Brethren, though I had done nothing against the people or the customs of our fathers, yet I was delivered prisoner from Jerusalem into the hands of the **Romans**. When they had examined me, they wished to set me at liberty, because there was no reason for the death penalty in my case. But when the Jews objected, I was compelled to appeal to Caesar — though I had no charge to bring against my nation. For this reason therefore I have asked to see you and speak with you, since it is because of the hope of Israel that I am bound with this chain."
> (Acts 28:14, 16–20; all emphases added)

Note how Paul is preaching to the Jews in **Rome**. This was his mission, his calling, his destiny. Without being Roman, Paul would have certainly been killed in Jerusalem for being a Christian. By being Roman, he was spared death until he got to Rome and was allowed Roman citizen privileges while under house arrest.

Acts 28:28–31 records, "'Let it be known to you then that this salvation of God has been sent to the Gentiles; they will listen.' And he lived there [**Rome**] two whole years at his own expense, and welcomed all who came to him, preaching the kingdom of God and teaching about the Lord Jesus Christ quite openly and unhindered." By the end of the book of Acts, Paul would preach unceasingly for at least two years in **Rome** about Jesus Christ. He would die a martyr. Because he was a Roman citizen, they could not crucify him according to Roman law. He was beheaded.

So, why does the book of Acts abruptly end when Paul gets to **Rome**? Because the Church has been established there, in the last empire that Daniel prophesied would fall — and from which Christianity would spread around the world.

Nevertheless, it would take another approximately 250 years from the martyrdom of Sts. Peter and Paul for God to fully convert the Roman Empire. In fact, it was Emperor Constantine who would finally convert the empire to Christianity when the Lord instructed him to take Rome via force and overthrow its evils. The Lord showed him the Cross and gave him the sign. Bishop Eusebius of Caesarea wrote of the Battle of Milvian Bridge, which took place on October 28 AD 312. Around noon, writes Eusebius, Constantine saw a luminous cross in the sky with the words *In hoc signo vinces*, meaning "In this sign thou shalt conquer." Constantine became the first emperor to convert to the Christian Church and in A.D. 313, he issued the Edict of Milan proclaiming freedom to practice Christianity.

The Lord placed Peter and Paul into the very belly of the beast, the Roman Empire. As a Roman citizen, Paul was free to speak, preach, and write until his death. In fact, Rome may have been his longest continuous stay in his ministry. While under house arrest in Rome, he wrote many of the epistles, or letters, of the New Testament. These include writings intended to strengthen the churches he established. They are to the Ephesians, Philippians, and Colossians. He also wrote his personal Letter to Philemon and wrote 2 Timothy, which would be his last written word before his execution. Many scholars place these writings somewhere around A.D. 62.

Paul's words in his famous Letter to the Romans — which many believe he wrote to the Church in Rome about A.D. 57, twenty-five years after the death and Resurrection of our Lord — clearly demonstrate the importance that he placed on this specific church, which he did not start and had not yet visited. In his own words:

> To all God's beloved in **Rome,** who are called to be saints: Grace to you and peace from God our Father and the Lord Jesus Christ. First, I thank my God through Jesus Christ for all of you, **because *your faith* is proclaimed in all the world**. (Rom. 1:7–8; all emphases added)

> So I am eager to preach the gospel to you also who are in **Rome**. (Rom. 1:15; emphasis added)

Notice how Paul makes claims about the Roman Church. It is the pinnacle of the New Testament world, only twenty-five years after the Resurrection. The Roman faith was the prized trophy and the finest fruit of the apostles and their travels. This compliment is not paid to any other city where believers lived. Also, note Paul's zeal to get to Rome to preach to them personally.

One may ask, is there any other proof that Sts. Peter and Paul went to Rome to establish Jesus' Church? Yes.

St. Irenaeus was bishop of Lyons from about A.D. 180–200. He is widely known as of one the greatest of the post-apostolic theologians of the immediate post-apostolic period. He received his training in theology from St. Polycarp, who was tutored by St. John the apostle himself. In his writing *Against Heresies*, St. Irenaeus made the following statement about the Church in Rome and the successors of St. Peter:

> But since it would be too long to enumerate in such a small volume as this the succession of all the **churches**, we shall confound all those who, in whatever manner, whether through self-satisfaction or vainglory, or through blindness and wicked opinion, assemble other than where it is proper, by pointing out here **the successions of the bishops of the greatest and most ancient Church known to all, founded and organized in Rome,** by the two most glorious apostles, Peter and Paul, **that Church which has the tradition and the faith** which comes down to me by the Apostles. **With that church,** because of its superior origin, **all the churches must agree, that is, all the faithful in the whole world, and it is in her that the faithful everywhere have maintained the apostolic tradition.**[2]

St. Irenaeus then went on to name all twelve popes who succeeded Peter up to his time.

In this same book, St. Irenaeus told us that Linus was the first successor of Peter as the Bishop of Rome. This is the same Linus that

---

[2] William A. Jurgens, *The Faith of the Early Fathers* vol. I (Collegeville: Liturgical Press, 1970), p. 90; all emphasis added.

Paul writes about in his final letter. In 2 Timothy 4:21, he states, "Do your best to come before winter. Eubulus sends greetings to you, as do Pudens and **Linus**, and Claudia and all the brethren" (emphasis added). By the time that St. John the apostle had died, the Church was into her fifth pope, inclusive of Peter. Regardless of the exact number of popes that were martyred in the early Church, one can say with certainty that before the end of the Roman persecution of the Church which ended around A.D. 313, every man who accepted the papacy did so with full knowledge that martyrdom was possible for him at any moment.

How the Church Handled Heresy

The Church fought heresies from day one. This is not a book about heresies from within the Church. But the reader may wish to study these to determine how the Church handled Gnosticism (ca. the second century), Arianism (ca. the third and fourth century), and Nestorianism (ca. the fifth century), to name just a few.

During these times, the Church held councils and reached consensus through the workings of the Holy Spirit to consider and rule on questions of doctrine, discipline, and other matters. These have included excommunication from the Church. One example of this that prominently lives on today is the origin of the Nicene Creed. The Nicene Creed was an outcome of the First Council at Nicaea in A.D. 325, which met very shortly after Emperor Constantine converted the Roman Empire to Christianity in A.D. 313.

The Catholic Church's bishops were confronting a heresy from within by Arius, a clergyman in the Alexandrian church. This became known as the Arian Heresy, or Arianism. Arius believed that Jesus was divine, but somehow less than God the Father. This notion was contrary to the idea of a triune God: one God in three Persons.

Nicene Creed

The Nicene Creed was the universal Church's way of creating a complete and uniform consensus in Jesus' Church on liturgy and prayer. It is how we worship one God in three Persons. It even expanded upon the Apostles' Creed which was written during the pontificate of Pope St. Eleutherus, who was martyred in A.D. 189. In A.D. 381, the Nicene Creed was adopted and authorized by Jesus' Church as the only true expression of faith at the Second Ecumenical Council of Constantinople in A.D. 381. All the words of this Creed can be sourced directly from Sacred Scripture. Some churches have modified the Creed, or developed their own, but the following is the actual text of the Creed developed by the universal Church, still used by the Catholic Church today.

The Nicene Creed: The Profession of Faith in Christ's Church

> I believe in one God, the Father almighty, maker of Heaven and earth, of all things visible and invisible.
>
> I believe in one Lord Jesus Christ, the Only Begotten Son of God, born of the Father before all ages. God from God, Light from Light, true God from true God, begotten, not made, consubstantial with the Father; through Him all things were made. For us men and for our salvation, He came down from Heaven, and by the power of the Holy Spirit was incarnate of the Virgin Mary, and became man. For our sake He was crucified under Pontius Pilate, He suffered death and was buried, and rose again on the third day in accordance with the Scriptures. He ascended into Heaven and is seated at the right hand of the Father. He

will come again in glory to judge the living and the dead and His Kingdom will have no end.

I believe in the Holy Spirit, the Lord, the giver of life, who proceeds from the Father and the Son, who with the Father and the Son is adored and glorified, who has spoken through the prophets.

I believe in one, holy, catholic, and apostolic Church. I confess one Baptism for the forgiveness of sins and I look forward to the resurrection of the dead and the life of the world to come. Amen.

This profession of faith is recited as a prayer in response to the proclamation of God's Word — the gospel message. It is part of every Sunday Mass and Divine Liturgy throughout the world.

The reader should remember its origin within Jesus' Church. It was a gift of the Holy Spirit to mankind to ensure defense against heresy, as Church laity profess this from their lips in unison. It also ensures that the universality of the Faith remains amongst all Catholic Christians to this very day.

Today, many churches which claim to be "Christian" do not accept or profess the Nicene Creed. Others simply eliminate sections, or add or edit the words. Still others accept the Apostles' Creed but not the Nicene Creed. But both the Apostolic and Nicene Creeds came from the Church that Christ established. They were given to the faithful to ensure universal beliefs in faith and authority of the Church in matters of faith. They were made to prevent heresies and to guard against false preachers crafting or creating their own belief system, their own theologies, and their own churches.

This is why the Nicene Creed ends with a common belief in *one, holy, catholic, and apostolic Church*. To be in Christ's Church, one must meet all four criteria. The Church must be *one* (same practices, liturgy, worship, etc.). She must be *holy*. This means that the Church herself is holy because God Himself, through Christ Jesus, established her and she is guided by the Holy Spirit until Jesus comes again. (Of course, people — including those inside His Church, including in her ecclesiastical hierarchy — are sinners and may or may not act holy. But the Church herself is *holy* because Jesus started her and promised the Holy Spirit to guide her.) In other words, the wheat and the tares must grow together until the Lord's return and harvest. The Church must be *catholic*. This means *universal* in every city, state, nation, continent, and throughout the world, regardless of changing nations, borders, and political interests. The Roman Empire was the known world at the time of Christ. Now Christianity is on every continent. This is fulfilling what the resurrected, glorified Jesus commanded of the apostles and their successors in Matthew 28:19–20:

> Go therefore and make disciples of all nations, baptizing them in the name of the Father and of the Son and of the Holy Spirit, teaching them to observe **all** that I have commanded you; and lo, I am with you always, to the close of the age. (emphasis added)

These instructions by Our Lord were given to the apostles. He also instructed them to teach *all* of His commandments, and not to develop their own theology. Thus, in historical context, the Great Commission was given to the apostles and their successors through the laying on of hands. They were to teach the fullness of Truth, governing and sanctifying the laity with the Word and the sacraments. No human founder of any subsequent faith or religion was present at the Great Commission.

Finally, the Church is *apostolic*. Christ Himself guaranteed that His Church, founded upon Peter as the chief shepherd along with the other apostles, would 1) never cease (He will be with them until the end of time) and 2) would never be prevailed upon by the gates of Hell.

The reader should pause and reflect on this question: Does my faith, do my beliefs, does my place of worship encompass all of the aspects of the Nicene Creed? If not, where is it lacking? And why?

Oral History Becomes Sacred Scripture

From A.D. 33 through A.D. 382, the story of the life and teachings of Jesus Christ, the Son of God, was being told mostly by word of mouth, known as oral tradition. The only writings were of the Church Fathers, most of whom were bishops of the Church. These writings provide us with some key definitional terms regarding the liturgy and procedures consistently used during the Holy Mass of the ancient Church. (Although not a topic we will cover in this book, we urge you to read about what the Church Fathers wrote to the churches principally during the first five centuries.)

As the Creed became formalized for every Christian throughout the Church, Pope Damasus I in A.D. 382 wrote a decree listing all the books that were determined to be of divine origin, that should be included in the Bible. There were a total of seventy-three sacred books. This was done at the Council of Rome. Then in A.D. 393, the Catholic Church ratified the present Old Testament and the New Testament books at the Council of Hippo in North Africa; again, seventy-three books. Finally, in A.D. 397, the Council of Carthage in

North Africa ratified the present Old and New Testament canon of seventy-three books.

The Bible was God-breathed by the Holy Spirit, working through men who were successors of Peter and the bishops of His Body, which is the Church, as St. Paul states such in 2 Timothy 3:16, where he uses the Greek word *theopneustos* (meaning "God-breathed"). The acceptance of the Bible as the authority within Christendom was profound. St. Augustine directly expressed his viewpoint on this by saying, "I would not believe in the Gospel, if the **authority of the Catholic Church** did not move me to do so."[3]

The Church after Jesus' Resurrection

We have just shown that Sacred Scripture reveals that Jesus founded the Catholic Church. He founded one, holy, catholic, and apostolic Church. Let's review where the word *church* appears now, after Jesus died and resurrected in Sacred Scripture.

Some of the more prominent uses of the word *church* appear from St. Paul's epistles. In all instances, Paul is very clear that Jesus' Church is also God the Father's Church. Let's look at some examples:

> Acts 8:1–3 states, "And on that day a great persecution arose against **the church** in Jerusalem; and they were all scattered throughout the region of Judea and Samaria, except the apostles. Devout men buried Stephen, and made great lamentation over him. But Saul laid waste **the church**, and entering house after house, he dragged off men and women and committed them to prison" (all emphases added). The apostolic Church is Jesus' Church.

---

[3] St. Augustine, *Epis. Contra. Man.*, 5:6; PL 42:176; emphasis added.

> 1 Corinthians 15:9 states, "For I [Paul] am the least of the apostles, unfit to be called an apostle, because **I persecuted the church of God**" (emphasis added). Paul acknowledges and confirms that the apostolic Church is God's true Church. Why does he call it God's Church and not Jesus' Church? Because Paul knew that it was God the Father who gave the divine revelation to Peter, as Jesus Himself says in the book of Matthew. St. Paul also recognizes who the leader of God's Church is. It is Peter. It is why Paul in his letters refers to Peter as *Cephas*, the Greek word for Peter — the new name that Christ Himself gave Peter.

Jesus then sent Paul to Ananias, who was the bishop of Damascus, appointed by Peter. Christ Himself told Ananias to lay hands on Paul, to heal him of his physical and more importantly his spiritual blindness. In addition, this act *conferred the Holy Spirit upon him through apostolic succession. Ponder this point:* Of all the apostles — of all missionaries, preachers, proclaimers of the gospel throughout history — Paul clearly had the greatest credentials of anyone to start his own church. But he didn't. He understood God's authority and simply joined the Church of God, which he wrote about in Sacred Scripture. Paul also obeyed Jesus' command to stop persecuting Him by Paul's destructive behavior against Christ's body. Let's note the words of Our Lord which Luke documents, Jesus' conversation with Paul at his conversion.

> Now as he (Paul) journeyed he approach Damascus, and suddenly a light from heaven flashed about him. And he fell to the ground and heard a voice saying to him, "Saul, Saul, why do you persecute *me*? And he said, "Who are you, Lord?" And he said, "*I am Jesus, whom you are persecuting.*" (Acts 9:3–5; emphasis added)

St. Paul understood that by persecuting Christ's Church, he was persecuting Jesus Himself. For this is what the Lord spoke to Paul. This is continued proof that Jesus' apostolic Church is of divine origin after Christ's Resurrection.

Let us move from Paul's acknowledgment of his sinning against the Church to his defining what God's Church is. Paul will call God's Church a "household."

In 1 Timothy 3:14–15, he writes, "I am writing these instructions to you so that, if I am delayed, you may know how one ought to behave in the **household of God, which is the church of the living God, the pillar and bulwark of the truth**" (emphasis added). There is only one Truth. It is God Himself in all three Persons; therefore, if God is Truth, then Paul tells us that His Church is the pillar and foundation of Truth. He also says that the living God dwells within this Church.

In Ephesians 2:19–22 he goes on to say, "So then you are no longer strangers and sojourners, but you are fellow citizens with the saints **and members of the household of God, built upon the foundation of the apostles and prophets, Christ Jesus himself being the cornerstone**, in whom the whole structure [this church household] is joined together and grows into a holy temple in the Lord; in whom you also are built into it for a dwelling place of God in the Spirit" (emphasis added).

Paul is telling us that God's Church is a household of members. Jesus is the capstone, meaning "head." But Paul adds a third definition of God's Church. Her foundation must be the apostolic Church. If you recall, we briefly described the New Jerusalem in the book of Revelation. St. John describes the eternal dwelling place for mankind — "The wall of the city had twelve **foundations, and on them the twelve names of the twelve apostles of the lamb**" (Rev. 21:14;

emphasis added). The Church is His Bride. She is apostolic, as both Sts. John and Paul write.

The Great Schisms

Until A.D. 1054, there was only one Church, only one Christendom. But then the East-West Schism occurred. There were a number of doctrinal disagreements between the Eastern patriarchates (Constantinople, Jerusalem, Alexandria, and Antioch) and Rome: the use of unleavened bread, the question of celibacy for clerics, the exact wording of the Nicene Creed, and the primacy of the pope. But the Schism was also caused by sociopolitical issues. In any case, when the Eastern Catholics broke communion with Rome, suddenly there were Eastern Christians, who called themselves Orthodox, and Western Christians, who called themselves Catholic.

Pope Leo IX excommunicated the Patriarch of Constantinople, Michael Cerularius. Constantinople then excommunicated Rome. Christ's Body was broken.

The Schism continues to this day. The current churches of the Eastern Schism are the Greek Orthodox and Russian Orthodox churches. They are the second largest classifications of Christians. They refer to themselves as "Eastern Orthodox," or more officially and correctly the "Orthodox Catholic Church." They represent approximately three hundred million baptized members.

A significant moment took place in 1965 when Pope St. Paul VI and Athenagoras I agreed to lift the excommunications of Leo IX and Michael Cerularius issued in 1054. Although this was an encouraging act of goodwill, full communion is not yet established. Old wounds take a long time to heal. There has been more and more cooperation regarding the recognition of the sacraments within both Eastern and Western churches, as well as mutual proclamations such as the Alexandria Document in 2023 that addressed the issues of synodality and primacy in the modern era. In fact, every year a delegation from each of the churches joins each other's patronal church feast days, Sts. Peter and Paul on June 29 for Rome and November 30 for St. Andrew in Constantinople.

Between A.D. 1378 and 1417, two and sometimes three people claimed to be the pope. This was caused by several cardinals arguing that the election of Pope Urban VI in 1378 was somehow coerced by hostile uprisings in Rome. This was known as the "Great Schism" within the Catholic Church herself, as factions formed, each with their constituencies.

However, this schism has healed. It ended with the election of Pope Martin V in 1417.

In time, God willing, the East-West schism will also heal. Once again, the Eastern and Western Churches will be as Jesus promised, and as the apostles promulgated: united in doctrine and dogma, one, holy, catholic, and apostolic Church (see John 17:21).

REFLECTIONS

1. Do you profess the Nicene Creed as your profession of faith? If not, why?

2. Did any member of the Most Holy Trinity after Jesus' Resurrection and Ascension ever commission *any* human being to make disciples of all nations, baptize, and teach people to observe and obey all of Jesus' teachings (see Matt. 28:19–20)?

3. Did Jesus give permanent power to the apostles to carry out His teachings? Was this power and authority intended for the successors of the apostles?

Chapter 3

Religious Revolution in Europe: The Triggering Event

St. Paul was undoubtedly prescient when he wrote these two texts:

> I am astonished that you are so quickly deserting him who called you in the grace of Christ and turning to a different gospel — not that there is another gospel, but there are some who trouble you and want to pervert the gospel of Christ. But even if we, or an angel from heaven, should preach to you a gospel contrary to that which we preached to you, let him be accursed. As we have said before, so now I say again, **if anyone is preaching to you a gospel contrary to that which you received [from Paul], let him be accursed!** (Gal. 1:6–9; emphasis added)

> Take heed to yourselves [the presbyters of the Church] and to all the flock, in which the Holy Spirit has made you guardians, **to feed the church of the Lord** which he obtained with his own blood. **I know that after my departure fierce wolves will come in among you**, not sparing the flock; and from among your own selves [bishops and clergy] will arise men speaking perverse things, to draw away the disciples after them. (Acts 20:28–30; all emphases added)

In Galatians, the context is that some members of the church that he established in Galatia had begun to stray from his teachings. St. Paul is very direct with his apostolic authority, directed at anyone who sought to "pervert" the gospel teachings that he laid down. Jewish Christians and Gentile Christians were in the same Church. The Jewish converts wanted to include circumcision, Sabbath observance, and observance of the Mosaic covenant, and as such, they were attempting to influence and change the doctrine that Paul had established and taught. St. Paul was very clear. Anyone who wished to change the doctrine of the gospel laid down by him was to be accursed. (In some texts, the word *anathema* is used rather than *accursed*, which means a formal curse that results in excommunicating a person and denouncing a false doctrine.)

St. Paul's recorded words above in chapter 20 of the book of Acts are most poignant. Although his immediate audience is the "ancients of the Church" in Ephesus, his prophetic words will ring loud and clear throughout the ages. There were many heretical priests, bishops, cardinals, and yes, even popes (Honorius I) during the Roman Catholic Church's history who would say things heretical to the Faith. For all have sinned and are deprived of the glory of God (Rom. 3:23) — including those called to the priesthood and religious life, the Church's very shepherds.

Paul states in the above Acts passage that he "knows" that some of the shepherds of the Church will pervert the Truth and draw disciples away from the Church, and that these men will insist that they follow them personally (as well as their teachings). He says that these men will be savage wolves in sheep's clothing, meaning not true shepherds. They will devour the flock and draw people away from the **Church of God**. They will come from within the priesthood of Jesus' Church herself.

The Protestant Reformation

In chapter 2, we briefly mentioned a few early attempts to redefine the doctrine of faith which came from within the Church, those of Arius (Arian Heresy) and Nestorius (Nestorian Heresy). Now we will discuss the creation of "state-churches" sanctioned by human law during the Protestant Reformation of A.D. 1517. There is no historically recognized divine origin of this human activity sponsored by the state.

The leader of the Protestant Reformation was an Augustinian priest named Martin Luther. Rather than reform the Church from within, he decided to attempt to reform her, on his terms, from the outside. He needed government officials as enablers, rather than the Holy Spirit.

Many books have been written to either defend or criticize his actions. This book will simply make some factual observations about what he accomplished.

To begin with, the fracturing of Western Christianity which he initiated accelerated dramatically. Indeed, different doctrines, religions, and faiths appeared almost immediately. For if any one man could create a set of religious beliefs and teachings and somehow make it socially acceptable, then any other man could do the same. The myriad of Christian denominations that we see today — Anglicans, Congregationalists, Presbyterians, Methodists, Baptists, Mormons, Adventists, Jehovah's Witnesses, Fundamentalists, Evangelicals, and more — can all trace their roots back to 1517 and what Fr. Luther did. And they keep splintering.

After Martin Luther, many other men would seize the opportunity to create their own churches, and indeed religions, by changing the meaning of Scripture or rewriting Sacred Scripture itself. Like Luther, they would also seize upon the human political power and national governments to gain power over the Roman Catholic Church. In addition, there has been much human turmoil caused by moving to man-made religions from divine origin. After Luther, some men were particularly adept at stepping forward to attempt to change the doctrine and theology of the one, holy, catholic, and apostolic Church. Some include Ulrich Zwingli, a former Swiss priest (Swiss Reformed Church, active around 1519), John Calvin, a French reformer (active from the late 1520s to early 1530s), and King Henry VIII in 1534, who passed the Act of Supremacy as king, thus making him the head of the new Church of England. What all these men had in common is they denounced that the Roman Catholic Church had authority from Christ. They wanted their followers to believe that they had full authority to create a church and thus a religion in the confines of their land kingdom.

King Henry VIII, in essence, created his own state-sponsored church so that he could divorce his wife and seek another wife — though the Catholic Church teaches that this is morally wrong, just as John the Baptist told King Herod, "It is not lawful [morally right in God's eyes] for you to have your brother's [ex-]wife" (Mark 6:18). King Henry VIII executed Catholic priests, seized Catholic monasteries, and persecuted Catholics. They were to denounce their Catholic Faith and submit to the king's new religion that was crafted by ordinary Protestant men under authority of the king and his army. In his hatred toward the Catholic Church, the king even ordered the execution of a Carthusian monk, Sebastian Newdigate, and the beheading of bishop and cardinal John Fisher for not supporting Henry's right to be the supreme head (authority above the Roman pontiff) of the Church of England. He personally ordered the executions of over sixty thousand people as king and the supreme leader of his church. We will study more about this tyrannical man in the next chapter.

Before Luther, the standard description of our Christian relationship with God was that God created man, Jesus created the Church, and the Church compiled the Bible. Luther conceived a new relationship: man determines doctrine, reinterprets the Bible accordingly, and a new church is created through an enabling government rule or law.

The following diagram depicts the consequences of this man-centered approach to Christian religion over human time:

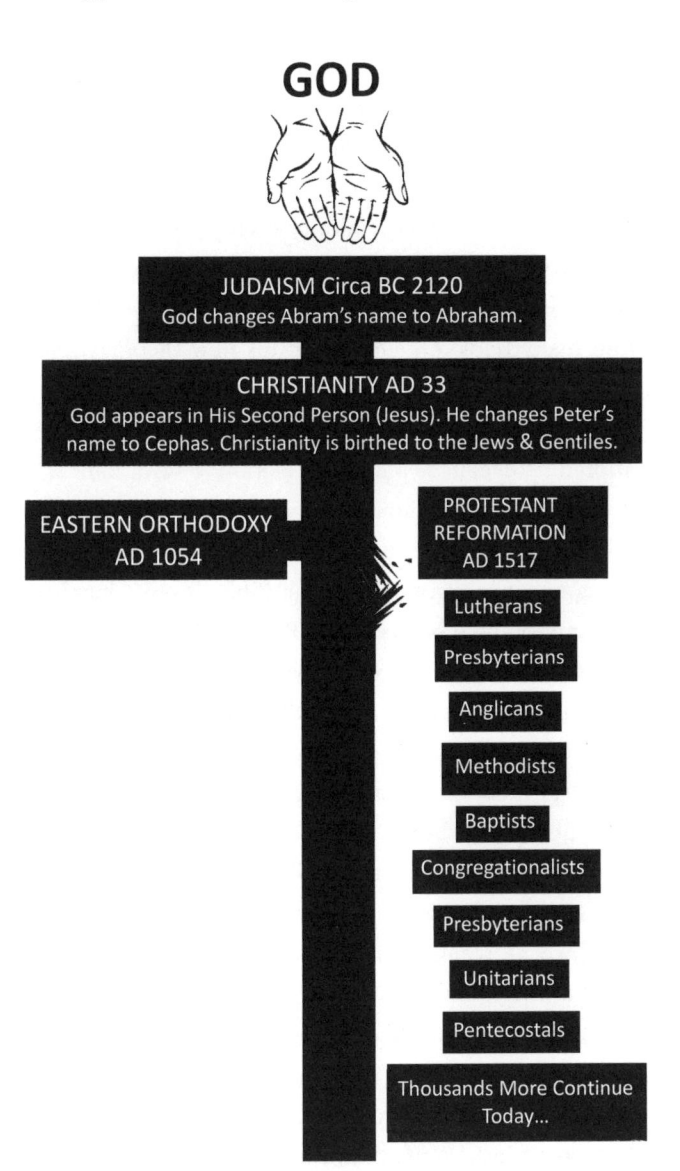

GOD

JUDAISM Circa BC 2120
God changes Abram's name to Abraham.

CHRISTIANITY AD 33
God appears in His Second Person (Jesus). He changes Peter's name to Cephas. Christianity is birthed to the Jews & Gentiles.

EASTERN ORTHODOXY AD 1054

PROTESTANT REFORMATION AD 1517

Lutherans

Presbyterians

Anglicans

Methodists

Baptists

Congregationalists

Presbyterians

Unitarians

Pentecostals

Thousands More Continue Today...

Of course, many of the Church reformers were understandably critical of Rome and the genuine clerical corruption within the Church. But corruption does not justify changes of theology. More importantly, hypocrisy does not nullify the truth.

Nevertheless, Luther unilaterally championed theological change. He systematically redefined redemption and grace. He introduced two new doctrines: *sola scriptura* (the Bible alone) and *sola fide* (justification by faith alone, absent any works). He even began the project of altering Sacred Scripture. In fact, a new Bible would emerge that eliminated certain books and edited the original text from many books in support of his new theology. He even wished to eliminate the Letter of James, which he called "an epistle of straw," as well as the book of Revelation, because both James and Revelation disprove his *sola fide* proposition to salvation.

He relented on the elimination of James and Revelation when others thought that it was too radical. However, he was successful in eliminating seven sacred books of the Bible. Jesus' Church recognized all seventy-three books of the Bible as canonical — meaning declared as the complete Word of God. Luther would declare seven of the original sacred texts as non-canonical — or somehow not inspired by God (see 2 Tim. 3:16). Here was a man, a former Catholic priest no less, who decided that he knew what a Bible should contain to support his opinion better than the Church. Again, there was no divine origin. This would be the most dangerous thing that Luther ever did, as it opened a Pandora's box for anyone else to do the same.

Today, we are reeling from human self-interpretation of Scripture. So, who is right and how can there be differing truths? What does divine revelation say? Do works matter? Can we add, delete, or change sacred text?

Consider these words from the Bible: **"And I heard a voice from heaven saying, 'Write this: Blessed are the dead who die in** the Lord henceforth.' 'Blessed indeed' says the Spirit, 'that they may rest from their labors, for their deeds [works] follow them!'" (Rev. 14:13; emphasis added). Works must matter to God because they will accompany you into the Kingdom.

"I warn every one who hears the words of the prophecy of this book: if any one adds to them, God will add to him the plagues described in this book, and if *anyone takes away from the words* of the book of this prophecy, God will take away his share in the tree of life and in the holy city, which are described in this book" (Rev. 22:18–19; emphasis added). The Bible is taken altogether as the inerrant Word of God. Although it comprises seventy-three separate writings, it is one book. Sadly today, especially in the United States, many Christians believe that the Bible only has sixty-six books! The damage that Martin Luther (and King James) did was immense.

Ironically, the first Bible ever printed was the Gutenberg Bible. It came about in the century *before* Luther started his Reformation. The seven books that he decided to eliminate are *included* in the first printed Bible for the masses of literate people. So again, what was Luther's real rationale and motivation for questioning seven books of the Bible and ultimately labeling them as "non-canonical"? They did not support his new man-made and personal theology of faith alone and the Bible alone.

Sadly, others in Europe soon followed suit and heresies swiftly multiplied, further dividing Christ's Body. Again, volumes have been written about Luther, both pro and con. But remember one thing: every man-made denomination in the world today stems from his attempt to change doctrine and his rejection of the apostolic authority given by Jesus to His Church.

Here is what you should know: scandal is nothing new for the Church. It always comes from within. Much of it is the devil himself always trying to divide, separate, cause strife, slow down the spread of Christianity, and instill hatred.

The Roman Catholic Church experienced great turmoil caused by the "Babylonian captivity of the papacy," which followed the Great Eastern Schism, when the pope moved from Rome to Avignon, France. This occurred from A.D. 1309 to 1377. During the Renaissance period, the Church became weakened by nationalism, humanism, and corruption of wealth and power. The evil of simony had invaded the Church. Some clergy in high offices would give favors or money, even to members of their own families (nepotism). Even the popes surrounded themselves with members of their families, providing them with high incomes from the Church. The Church was in dire need of renewal, but it appeared as though the Church would have to be chastised before she could be renewed. Let's look at the immediate time period within the Church leading up to the protest by Luther.

Worldliness of the Renaissance Popes

Three worldly popes would pave the way for Luther's revolt. Although some reforms were attempted in the late Middle Ages, the Renaissance popes were themselves obstacles to the renewal of the Church. Indeed, because the Church hierarchy was often comprised of nobles and wealthy families, the Church was suffering from a lack of holy popes.

Alexander VI, the Spaniard who became pope in 1492, was political-minded, not spiritual. He desired to make his family (the Borgias) the most powerful in Italy and all of Europe. He loved luxury. He lived in lavishly decorated dwellings. He would even bring his illegitimate children to the Vatican without embarrassment!

In 1503, Alexander VI died and an elderly pope, Pius III (who would live but only a few weeks), would succeed him. So the next pope of consequence was Julius II. He was focused on uniting Italy under the papacy itself. His skills were diplomacy and military war operations rather than Church reformation.

The third worldly pope, Leo X, would succeed him in 1513. His primary interest was in art rather than spiritual matters. In the age of the Renaissance, he too was worldly, materialistic, and he sought fine art continuously. He did very little to provide reforms from within.

Simultaneously, these popes were faced with the rise of nationalism occurring in Europe. Princes and kings would allow reforms of the Church within their territories for a price. The popes and the Church were forced to negotiate concordats or treaties with these nations. These nations made vast sums of money by manipulating the Church. As papal expenses to these nations grew, revenues were under stress. This age saw many secular rulers themselves become prelates for monetary gain and control. The Church tried to levy papal taxes on these men for their ecclesiastical offices. In essence, high positions in the Church came at a steep price, but these noblemen could afford it. This morally corrupt practice of selling spiritual goods and offices in the Church is the sin of simony. It has categorically been condemned by the Church.

The immoralities of Pope Alexander VI, Pope Julius II, and Pope Leo X were self-evident. Although none of them taught heresy per se, they were not moral leaders. The lack of spiritual leadership from these three popes, coupled with the lack of sound teachings from the Catholic clergy, allowed the common layman to fall prey to Luther's new religion.

Some prelates and princes encouraged the pope to call an ecumenical council to reform the Church. In 1512, Pope Julius II reluctantly called the Fifth Lateran Council in Rome. It didn't conclude until 1517, on the eve of Luther's Protestant Reformation under Pope Leo X. Many decrees to reform the Church were passed.

However, the worldliness of the pope caused by his lack of spiritual vision prevented the implementation of most of the council's decrees. The council's recommendations could only be successful if they were personally driven by the pope himself. The success of the Protestant Reformation was due largely to the fact that real reform was never implemented by the popes.

The greatest European scholar at the time was Erasmus of Rotterdam (1465–1536). He was a priest and theologian. He tried to reform the Church using the Church Fathers and Scripture, but his erudition was not enough. He was a patient man, knowing that God was allowing this for His good. He urged Luther to cease his unilateral actions to create a new religion. Luther would continue his self-destructive behavior, and when the highly respected Erasmus died in 1536, Luther publicly condemned this holy man by saying, **"The famous Erasmus has died in Basel, without a priest or prayers, ready for hell"** (emphasis added). No human being has the right to say such a thing about another man — especially a holy one.

Martin Luther

Martin Luther, a thirty-four-year-old monk from a German order, lived during a spiritually anemic period of the Church. The Catholic Church was spiritual firewood and Luther was the spark. Luther was born to poor parents in Eisleben (Saxony) in 1483. His father wanted him to be a lawyer, but he pursued the life of a monk. This was caused when a bolt of lightning threw him to the ground in 1505 while he was attending the University of Erfurt. He vowed that he would enter the Monastery of the Hermits of St. Augustine if God spared his life.

Written records indicate that he received his doctorate in Scripture in 1512. He taught classes at the University of Wittenberg from 1515 to 1516. Luther was an academic. He was enamored with finding one verse of the Bible to define him. Romans 1:17 states, "For in it the righteousness of God is revealed through faith for faith; as it is written, '**He who through faith is righteous shall live**'" (emphasis added). The Scripture referred to in this verse from the Letter to the Romans is from Habakkuk 2:4. Luther isolated this passage, and it would become "the gate to paradise" in his mind. There was no divine revelation, no voice from Heaven, nor angelic messengers. Just his voice in his mind.

A rule of the Augustinian Order that he followed in his training was to read Scripture assiduously, hear it devoutly, and learn it frequently. However, as a monk, Luther did not find the assurance of salvation, the peace of mind, or the rest of the soul that he desperately sought.

Scholars generally agree that Luther suffered from a mental or neurotic disorder called *scrupulosity*, which affected not only his thinking and behavior but also his theology. Scrupulosity is a subset of obsessive-compulsive disorder involving religious or moral obsession. Individuals who suffer from scrupulosity are overly concerned that something that they thought or did might be a sin or violation of religious or moral doctrine. Scrupulosity produces constant feelings of doubt, guilt, and anxiety. It typically produces feelings and thoughts of seeing mortal sin where there is only venial sin. It also manifests in obsessively focusing on the possibility of imaginary sins that may not be sinful at all. Scrupulosity, in the Roman Catholic Church's moral teaching, is defined as the spiritual and psychological state of a person who erroneously believes that he is guilty of mortal sin and therefore is seldom in a state of grace. Such a person never experiences serenity of conscience and peace of soul.

Luther's mental condition led him to believe that men are basically evil, totally depraved, and thus incapable of doing good. His personal mental disorder of scrupulosity would be projected upon his belief system and shared with his followers. We will study this via some infamous quotes of his. The words of the Bible were his only source of hope for his damning thinking. Although he believed that man is basically and intrinsically evil, he also believed that God did send His Son, Jesus, as Lord and Savior, to die for all mankind, rise from the dead, and ascend into Heaven, and that by accepting Christ's atonement by faith alone one is saved. On the surface, this sounds like correct teaching. But then he came to the theological conclusion that man is justified by faith alone and not by good works. You simply needed to be **righteous by faith — and salvation was yours**. Harken back to Romans 1:17, which is Luther's source and wellspring of his personal theology. In fact, he called it "the gate of paradise." However, Luther had a Scripture quote that stood in his way to faith alone within Romans — Romans 3:28. St. Paul is clear as he wrote: "For we hold that a man is justified by faith apart from works of the law." Luther changed Sacred Scripture by adding the word *alone*, placing it after the word "faith" in his German translation of the Bible. All Bibles prior to Luther including the Greek manuscripts do not contain "faith alone." Luther also assumed that if you have faith in Jesus Christ, good actions will naturally follow, and God will save you.

Indeed, the Church has always taught that only God can save a person and that man cannot save himself. Yet, this is how "faith alone" or *sola fide* was born as a new theology. Luther had a phobia of personal eternal damnation, afflicted by his mental disorder, which drove him to redefine the study of soteriology. This is the study of doctrines of salvation or salvation theories. Because he struggled so severely with his own shame and guilt, he concluded that "faith alone" must be sufficient. This belief became his formal principle of the Reformation. Luther suffered great desperation due to his view of his sinfulness. This led to his false doctrine. Since his good works did not give him any internal peace, he concluded that good works are useless for salvation. This stemmed from his false mental model that man is incapable of willing or doing anything good by his actions due to the consequences of Original Sin.

In essence, Luther thought that man cannot bear fruit because, due to our Original Sin, the tree and its fruits have all rotted. All man's actions are thus sinful. If one believes that man's works, actions, and deeds are inherently evil or sinful, salvation by faith alone fits perfectly. This self-professed doctrine must also include the thinking that works do nothing for salvation. So, if it is by "faith alone" that one is somehow (justified) saved, then one is free to sin, since it is man's nature to do so. One's actions or deeds in the body while alive on earth don't really matter at all.

Many Protestants simply say, "Hey! Look at the thief on the Cross next to Jesus — Jesus saved him!" But even the thief performed the "work" of speaking his faith out loud. Works, and every human action, do matter to our salvation. By our works, we will be judged at the end of our lives by Christ. St. Paul makes this clear: "For we must *all* appear before the judgment seat of Christ, so that each one may receive good or evil, according to what **he has done in the body**" (2 Cor. 5:10; all emphases added).

Luther's doctrine of "justification by faith alone" has never been taught in the history of Christendom by the Roman Catholic or Eastern Orthodox churches. Rather, what has been taught from the beginning is that Jesus' death on the Cross merited grace for us, and this grace via Baptism made us "new men and women" so that we may cooperate with full knowledge and a deliberate act of our free will. If we perform good works in a state of grace, it is meritorious for our soul and thus our salvation (see Matt. 25:34–36). This is possible because of our unity with Christ Himself (Col. 1:18).

Since Luther was, in essence, a victim of scrupulosity, he saw nothing in himself but wickedness and corruption. This was his self-view. It is why he proclaimed his conclusion of justification by faith alone. The mode of justification or being made righteous before God didn't matter to him. One verse in the Bible coupled with his neurosis became his theology. Think of it this way: Luther believed and taught that nothing that we do on earth truly has any merit at all, that we can neither earn grace nor become holier. He was counting on the idea that God would take even evil men into His presence provided that they simply believe in Christ. In fact, he told everyone not to worry about sin at all, because faith alone will save you. Here are some of his quotes concerning his view on God, the Ten Commandments, and how good works are sinful, and even, sin itself:

> I look upon God no better than a scoundrel.[4]

> I have greater confidence in my wife and my pupils than I do in Christ.[5]

> It is more important to guard against good works than against sin.[6]

> We must remove the Decalogue [the Ten Commandments of God] out of sight and heart.[7]

---

[4] *D. Martin Luthers Werke: kritische Gesammtausgabe*, 120 vols. (Weimar: Hermann Böhlau: 1883–2009), vol. 1, p. 487, hereafter "Weimar ed."; cf. *Table Talk*, no. 963.
[5] Luther, Martin. *Table Talk*, no. 2397b.
[6] *Table Talk*, Wittenberg ed., vol. 6. p. 160.
[7] *Briefe, Sendschreiben und Bedenken*, ed. W. M. L. de Wette, 6 vols. (1825–1856), vol. 4, p. 188, hereafter "de Wette ed."

If we allow them [the Ten Commandments] — any influence in our conscience, they become the cloak of all evil, heresies and blasphemies.⁸

Good works are bad and are sin like the rest.⁹

With regard to God, and in all that bears on salvation or damnation, (man) has no "free will," but is a captive, prisoner and bond slave, either to the will of God, or to the will of Satan.¹⁰

There is no scandal greater, more dangerous, more venomous than a good outward life, manifested by good works and a pious life. That is the grand portal, the highway that leads to damnation.¹¹

Be a sinner, and let your sins be strong, but let your trust in Christ be stronger.... No sin can separate us from Him, even if we were to kill or commit adultery thousands of times each day.¹²

Do not ask anything of your own conscience; and if it speaks, do not listen to it; if it insists, stifle it, amuse yourself;

---

⁸ O'Hare, Patrick. *The Facts about Luther*. Gastonia, NC: TAN Books, 1987, p. 311.
⁹ *Luther et Luthéranisme, Étude Faite d'après les sources*, ed. Henri Denifle, vol. 3, trans. J. Paquier (Paris: Picard, 1912–1913), p. 47.
¹⁰ From the essay "Bondage of the Will," in *Martin Luther: Selections From His Writings*, ed. John Dillenberger (New York: Anchor Books, 1962), p. 190.
¹¹ *De Servo Arbitrio*, 7, 113ff., quoted by Patrick F. O'Hare, in *The Facts About Luther* (TAN Books, 1987), pp. 266–267.
¹² "Let Your Sins Be Strong: A Letter from Luther to Melanchthon," Letter no. 99, August 1, 1521, in *Dr. Martin Luther's Saemmtliche Schriften*, ed. Johannes Georg Walch (St. Louis: Concordia, n.d.), vol. 15, cols. 2585–2590, trans. for Project Wittenberg by Erika Bullmann Flores, https://www.projectwittenberg.org/pub/resources/text/wittenberg/luther/letsinsbe.txt.

if necessary, commit some good big sin, in order to drive it away. Conscience is the voice of Satan, and it is necessary always to do just the contrary of what Satan wishes."[13]

In essence, he believed that man has a propensity to sin and that his nature is to do evil. He considered man's will insufficient to overcome concupiscence; and if he sins often, then faith alone is sufficient to save him (salvation).

The Church, however, teaches that free will is a gift from the Creator and that man either cooperates with God's grace or rejects it and sins. If one cooperates with God's grace, especially through the sacraments of the Church, then he is justified or made righteous. By aligning our free will with God's will for our lives, we become sanctified. Our works, while living in a state of grace, are meaningful to God, as we will produce fruit for the Kingdom "on earth" as it is in Heaven. So, even if man's concupiscence gives him the propensity to sin, he should not commit sins — especially mortal sins, which lead to death (see Rom. 6:23).

Given Luther's serious mental condition, one can readily see why he tells us to **sin and keep sinning ("murder and adultery a thousand times a day" — really?) because Jesus will somehow save you, because you acknowledge Him. Willful mortal sin is separation from God** (see Isa. 59:2).

How could a rational man say such things? Well, it is easy if one feels so very wretched about himself given his condition. To find any peace of mind, *sola fide* is the solution if one constantly feels guilt and shame, particularly if unwarranted. This is the mind of a scrupulous person. May we recall that Jesus Himself says, "Go and sin no more," along with, "Be perfect as my Heavenly Father is perfect." Jesus

---

[13] J. Döllinger, *La Réforme et les résultats qu'elle a produits*, vol. 3, trans. E. Perrot (Paris: Gaume, 1848–1849), p. 248.

makes His expectation clear — to avoid sin. Luther says the opposite. All deeds we perform are "works." Every action, decision, indecision, choice, or deliberate act of the will is a "work." These works will follow us at death (see Rev. 14:13).

The Ninety-Five Theses

Let us explain the context as to why Luther wrote his *Ninety-Five Theses* or *Disputation on the Power and Efficacy of Indulgences*. Hopefully, you will see that these were an overreaction on Luther's part, based upon 1) his scrupulous personality, and 2) the moral state of the leadership of the Church.

Pope Julius II was attempting to rebuild St. Peter's Basilica, so he offered a plenary indulgence to those who would contribute alms along with the reception of the sacraments. Remember that tithing to the Church is a biblical mandate (see 2 Cor. 8:1–4; 9:5–13). However, the men in the Church did abuse this mandate: the Church was wrought with nobility who would use their wealth to influence the elections of bishops and cardinals. A real example of this is as follows:

Jakob Fugger was a wealthy German merchant, entrepreneur, and banker from Mainz. His family had a legacy of wealth. Their companies grew significantly, as they had banking transactions with the House of Habsburg as well as the Roman Curia (the administration of the Holy See in Rome). Fuggar was also a cleric. He controlled the family empire and had a very powerful influence on European politics at the time.

Fuggar, who was a lifelong Catholic, made a loan to try and persuade the Roman Curia to approve the election of Albert of Brandenburg as the archbishop of Mainz. Unfortunately, Albert did not meet the canonical criteria. Albert suggested to Pope Leo X that a special indulgence be announced in his three dioceses in addition to his native diocese of Brandenburg. One-half of the income would go to the construction of the new St. Peter's Basilica in Rome and the other half would repay Fugger for the loan. The indulgence was entrusted to Albert in 1517 for publication in Saxony and Brandenburg.

Albert, the archbishop of Mainz, employed Johann Tetzel, a Dominican priest, for the actual preaching about the indulgence. Tetzel did this task horribly and misrepresented the Church's position by failing to explain the indulgence and the spiritual conditions required. Martin Luther, the Augustinian monk, was outraged at the Dominican priest, Tetzel, and challenged him to a debate concerning the indulgences. Historical fact: this occurred in one diocese in Germany only. It was not a universal Catholic Church uprising worldwide.

Luther posted his *95 Theses* on the chapel door at Wittenberg on October 31, 1517. This was a standard medieval way to challenge another academic to a debate. When Luther's bishop and Tetzel's bishop refused to respond to Luther, he made his *95 Theses* and his challenge public outside the Church.

Pope Leo X was informed by the archbishop of Mainz of this disturbance within Germany. The pope thought it was a simple feud between two monks of two different religious orders. The cat was out of the bag, so to speak. Luther renounced any good works to gain salvation or the remission of sin, including indulgences.

Luther Challenges the Church

Eventually, a meeting occurred between the papal legate, Cardinal Cajetan, and Luther at Augsburg in the autumn of 1518. Cajetan and Luther argued concerning the supremacy of faith alone (the new theology that Luther had invented) versus the relation of faith, works, and the sacraments of the Church which had always been taught. The meeting went nowhere, and Luther went away, but also dropped another ominous bomb; he questioned papal authority and thus Church authority.

Meanwhile, in Rome, the pope was embroiled in other worldwide political matters. This gave Luther about two years to preach, teach, write, and garner the support of the German people. He presented them with his alternative Christian theology with the sole goal of supplanting the teachings of the one, holy, catholic, and apostolic Church based in Rome.

To continue his protest, he added that he denied apostolic succession because the Church had been corrupted. Furthermore, he denigrated the Church and claimed that she was somehow not divinely founded as an institution but rather a human and historical group of communities of believers. He also challenged the papacy and Catholic priests, since he denounced hierarchy, and boldly proclaimed that everyone was a priest.

This came to a head in July 1519, in a theological debate in Leipzig between John Eck, a German Catholic theologian, and Martin Luther. In this debate, Luther publicly admitted that he did not believe in the divine origin of the Church nor papal primacy (the belief that the Bishop of Rome, the pope, is the universal supreme head of the Catholic Church). He also publicly denounced the infallibility of all the ecumenical councils of the Church.

Luther became his own "authority." He claimed *sola scriptura* — the Bible alone — as his supreme authority, yet the Bible itself contradicts this theology both directly and indirectly. By rejecting the divine origin and the apostolic teachings and Church Fathers, he was free to support his new soteriology based upon his human, revised Bible.

This left the Church no other option but excommunication. In 1520, Pope Leo X excommunicated Luther and denounced the forty-one false doctrines that he taught. The pope did call upon

Luther and gave him sixty days to recant. Luther refused to take back one single word. Luther began name-calling and claimed that the pope was the antichrist himself. The Protestant Revolt, known as the Protestant Reformation, was in full force. In defiance of the Church, on December 20, 1520, Luther along with his students and other supporters, burned the pope's bull *Exsurge Domine* along with a copy of the Church's canon law.

Many people have surmised that Luther's fundamental issue was his disdain for man's "free will," as his thinking was geared toward all things sinful due to his psychological condition. In believing that man cannot do good works (we are prone to evil), he concluded that good works cannot be involved in our salvation at all. Most people who study the facts of what Luther did in Germany conclude that it was his hubris and pride that got the better of him. He was not successful in getting the Church to acknowledge his *95 Theses*. His fundamental issue was with the authority of the Church which God created upon Christ and His apostles.

Luther Founds His Own Religion

Luther was a man without a Church, but he still had a country. He was determined to build his own religion. He wrote three pamphlets: 1) *An Address to the Nobility of the German Nation*, 2) *The Babylon Captivity of the Church*, and 3) *Freedom of a Christian*. The first was to gain favor and financing from the German populace. The second was an account of his false teachings about overall Church corruption, denial of priesthood, and denial of the power of the sacraments. The third pamphlet continued the attack against the Church's sacramental system, her devotions, the doctrine of justification (faith and works), and his appeal of faith alone — *sola fide*.

Much of what Luther said about the moral failings of the Catholic Church's dioceses in Germany was true; however, he portrayed these as failures of the entire Catholic Church. Luther, by denying Jesus' divine choosing of certain men to establish His Church, claimed that Jesus' choice to share His authority and power with these men was somehow now false, null and void. He had sealed his own fate. He had become an obstinate heretic to what the Church had taught since Christ Himself was in the flesh.

Emperor Charles V, whose vast empire included the Holy Roman Empire, summoned Luther on January 21, 1521. The emperor ordered him to stand trial and guaranteed him safe passage. Luther was asked if he indeed wrote books against the Church and her teachings. Luther affirmed this and refused to retract his doctrines. Luther was declared an outlaw and his books were ordered to be censored and destroyed. However, many principalities in central and northern Germany created their own state-churches under his influence. Western Christendom had become a house divided. From this single act of one man, many other mere mortals would start their own Christian religions. Depending on how one counts and assimilates the splintering of Protestantism, we now have over forty thousand denominations.

No man can judge the soul of another. God will judge all of us, including Luther. However, let us be reminded of Jesus' words in the Gospels of both Matthew and Luke, where He talks about how we will know a tree by its fruit. First, in Luke 6:45, He says, "The good man out of the good treasure of his heart produces good, and the evil man out of his evil treasure produces evil; **for out of the heart his mouth speaks**" (emphasis added). Furthermore, the Lord says in Matthew 12:36–37, **"I tell you, on the day of judgment men will render account for every careless word they utter; for by your** words you will be justified, and by your words you will be condemned"** (emphasis added).

Luther's Writings

We will conclude this chapter with some more revealing quotes from Martin Luther. It is often said that one can discern a man's character not only by his actions but also by his words.

Luther was counting on the peasants or common folk, and the Jews in Germany, to convert to his new religion. When they didn't, his tone changed dramatically—and he moved to systemically eliminate them! This behavior shows how much pride Luther possessed in himself. Whether with Rome and the papacy, the peasants, or the Jews, when Luther didn't get the outcome he wanted, he would verbally preach death and destruction to all opponents. Those who didn't accept and conform to his new theology were the enemies of his state-church.

In Luther's own words: "Christ committed adultery first of all with the woman at the well about whom St. John tells us. Was not everybody about Him saying; 'Whatever has he been doing with her?' Secondly, with Mary Magdalen, and thirdly with the woman taken in adultery whom He dismissed so lightly. Thus even, Christ who was so righteous, must have been guilty of fornication before He died."[14] This is from a man who wants us all to believe in *sola scriptura*! The Bible does not say any of this. This is simply blasphemy and hypocrisy on his part.

"To kill a peasant is not murder; it is helping to extinguish the conflagration. Let there be no half measures! Crush them! Cut their throats! Transfix them. Leave no stone unturned! To kill a peasant is to destroy a mad dog! If they say that I am very hard and merciless,

---

[14] *Table Talk*, in Weimar ed., vol. 2, p. 107.

mercy be damned. Let whoever can stab, strangle and kill them like mad dogs."[15] God's fifth commandment is "Thou shalt not kill." Yet *sola scriptura* again?

"[Luther] gave vent to the angry threat that, should he find another pious Jew to baptise he would take him to the bridge over the Elbe, hang a stone round his neck and push him over with the words: I baptise thee in the name of Abraham."[16] Did Luther forget that Jesus was a Jew? Along with His Mother and the Twelve? Didn't Christ Himself say that "salvation is from the Jews" (John 4:22)?

Yet, Luther persists:

> My advice, as I have said earlier, is: First, that their synagogues be burned down, and that all who are able toss sulphuric and pitch; it would be good if someone could also throw in some hellfire.... Second, that all their books — their prayer books, their Talmudic writings, also the entire Bible — be taken from them, not leaving one leaf, and that these be preserved for those who may be converted [to Luther's religion].... Third, that they be forbidden on pain of death to praise God, to give thanks, to pray, and to teach publicly among us and in our country.... Fourth, that they be forbidden to utter the name of God within our hearing. For we cannot with a good conscience listen to this or tolerate it.... He who hears this name [God] from a Jew must inform the authorities, or else throw sow dung at him when he sees him and chase him away."[17]

[15] Erlangen ed. (1826–1932), vol. 24, p. 294.
[16] Hartmann Grisar, S.J., *Luther*, ed. Luigi Cappadelta, trans. E. M. Lamond, vol. 5 (London: Paul, Trench, Trübner: 1916), p. 413.
[17] Martin Luther, *On the Jews and Their Lies*, trans. Martin H. Bertram (Minneapolis, MN: Fortress Press, 1955).

When the Jews didn't convert to his Lutheran teachings and theology, he wrote *On the Jews and Their Lies* to give a solution to the Jewish "problem" in Germany. Notice how he demands the burning of the synagogues, destruction of the Jewish sacred Old Testament literature (the Bible), cessation of their worship of God, and the reporting of Jews to the state authority. Also, in this writing, he states that rabbis are immediately forbidden to teach or suffer the pain of loss of life or limb. Additionally, he taught that all cash and treasure of gold or silver ought to be taken from the Jews.

Any sensible Christian today who hears these words spoken by a purported Christian man would rebuke him and not follow his teachings, for they are blasphemous. Luther could say and write these things because of his state-church sponsorship. All his proposed activities were designed to stop the Jewish people from practicing their religion and to extinguish their faith in God. No books, no teachings, no places of worship, no people, no race: this is the seed of German anti-Semitism. Its planter was Luther, and four centuries later, it would be Hitler and the Nazi party who would effectuate these ideas:

"It is not in opposition to the Holy Scriptures for a man to have several wives."[18] Really? This is clearly in opposition to the Word of God and is heresy.

"If the husband is unwilling, there is another who is; if the wife is unwilling, then let the maid come."[19] The Bible is clear that no adulterer or fornicator shall inherit the Kingdom of Heaven. Luther was overruling God's sixth commandment.

"What harm could it do if a man told a good lusty lie in a worthy cause and for the sake of the Christian Churches?"[20] Wasn't it God

---

[18] de Wette ed., vol. 2, p. 459.
[19] *Of Married Life*.
[20] *Briefwechsel*, ed. Max Lenz, vol. 1, p. 373. Also Grisar's Luther IV, p. 51

who said, "Thou shall not bear false witness"? Luther is tossing out God's eighth Commandment.

"St. Augustine and St. Ambrose cannot be compared with me."[21] "What I teach and write remains true even though the whole world should fall to pieces over it."[22] Evidently, Martin Luther was not a humble man. He said that he was superior to both Sts. Augustine and Ambrose. He also states that what he says and teaches is "truth" and will remain true even if the entire world falls apart over his teachings and writings. These are statements from a troubled man whose hubris and pride are blinding him. He is not the Truth; he cannot even teach or write the truth. His own words are contrary to God's Word and the Bible itself.

"To my mind, it [the book of Revelation] bears upon it no marks of an apostolic or prophetic character.... Everyone may form his own judgment of this book; as for myself, I feel an aversion to it, and to me this is sufficient reason for rejecting it."[23] Theologians accept that St. John the apostle wrote the book of the Apocalypse by divine revelation from Jesus Himself. Here, Luther said otherwise. He also said that it has no prophetic character. He continued to claim that everyone can self-interpret this book and have their own opinions. Clearly, he had such a strong "aversion to it" that he concluded by totally "rejecting it."

Of course, Satan too would have "had an aversion" to what Jesus had St. John write. Satan has reason and rejects God. We know how the Bible ends. God wins and Satan and his minions lose. Christ conquers. That is how our Bible ends. The story of mankind from the beginning to the end. Only in the book of Revelation do we see

---

[21] Erlangen ed., vol. 61, p. 422.
[22] Weimar ed., vol. 18, p. 401.
[23] O'Hare, Patrick. *The Facts about Luther*. Gastonia: TAN Books, 1987. pp. 169–170.

and understand Christ's final return and the victory He won for us. Why would Luther find no value in this triumphant ending for Christ the King of kings and Lord of lords? This is a question that one should ponder in their heart. Only in Revelation are we assured by the writings of Jesus' return and the marriage of His Bride, the Church, to Himself, the Bridegroom.

Yet, Martin Luther stated that he found no prophetic character to it, had a strong dislike of its contents, and rejected it. Satan would share his opinion, for he too rejected God's divine authority:

> If your Papist annoys you with the word [faith *"alone"* from Rom. 3:28], tell him straightaway, Dr. Martin Luther will have it so [Luther added the word *alone* after the word *faith* to the Bible in support of his new theology]: Papist and ass are one and the same thing. Whoever will not have **my translation**, let him give it the go-by: the devil's thanks to him who censures it *without **my** will and* **knowledge**. Luther will have it so, and he is a doctor above all doctors in Popedom."[24]

Martin Luther here acknowledges that he added text to support his self-proclaimed doctrine of justification by "faith alone," *sola fide*. In his arrogance, he calls the pope an "ass." He also admits that this is his own translation; therefore, it is of human origin and not of divine revelation. He also appeals to his self-will and knowledge that it is to be so. Lastly, he says that he is a "doctor" of the Church above all doctors of the Church. This self-proclamation of his superiority to all the doctors of the Church is staggering hubris. Doctors of the Church are saints recognized only by the Catholic Church. There have only

---

[24] *Amic. Discussion*, 1, 127, in *The Facts About Luther*, p. 201; all emphases added.

been thirty-seven human beings who have received this title for advancing the cause of Christ and His Church.

Martin Luther was a man on a mission who was justified in asserting that there were moral issues within the Catholic Church regarding indulgences. The sinful men within the Church will have to answer to God alone for their actions. However, he was incorrect to conclude that the Church's theology as it relates to faith needed to be changed to support his mental model altered by scrupulous neurosis. He sold this manipulation of Scripture and theology as a "reformation" of Christ's Church from A.D. 33 to A.D. 1517. The vitriolic nature of his words should cause one to wonder who could iterate these things, let alone place them as written words! This is the founder of Protestantism and its subsequent descendant churches. Just the facts.

As we close this chapter of the human history of Christendom, let us stick to the knitting regarding what Sacred Scripture teaches about one's tongue and the words it produces. For a man who proclaimed *sola scriptura*, perhaps he skimmed over the following words from the sacred text or simply decided to ignore them. St. James reminds us that any teacher of God's Word within the Church must know the important role and use of words. He gives us both good and bad uses of one's tongue as the chief instrument of teaching God's Word. The Christian message is conveyed by human words and the tongue is either God-focused (wisdom) or worldly focused (sinful self). A wise man watches his words:

> Know this, my beloved brethren. Let every man be quick to hear, slow to speak, slow to anger, for the anger of man does not work the righteousness of God.... But be doers of the word, and not hearers only, deceiving yourselves....
> If any one **thinks he is religious and does *not* bridle his**

> **tongue but deceives his heart, this man's religion is vain**. Religion that is pure and undefiled before God and the Father is this: to visit orphans and widows in their affliction, [these were the peasants in James's and Luther's time] and to keep **oneself unstained from this world**. (James 1:19–20, 22, 26–27; all emphases added)

"To keep oneself unstained from this world" is to not be drawn into sin by your own free will — yet Luther says that sin is normal and permissible.

Furthermore, from James:

> So the tongue is a little member and boasts of great things. How great a forest is set ablaze by a small fire! **And the tongue is a fire. The tongue is an unrighteous world among our members, staining the whole body, setting on fire the cycle of nature, and set on fire by hell.** For every kind of beast and bird, of reptile and sea creature, can be tamed and has been tamed by humankind, but no human being can tame the tongue — a restless evil, full of deadly poison. With it we bless the Lord and Father, and with it we **curse men**, who are made in the likeness of God. From the same mouth come blessing and cursing. My brethren, this ought not be so.... Who is wise and understanding among you? By his good life let him show his works in the meekness of wisdom. But if you have bitter jealousy and selfish ambition in your hearts, **do not boast and be false to the truth. This wisdom is not such as comes down from above, but is earthly, unspiritual, devilish. For where jealousy and selfish ambition exist, there will be disorder and every vile practice.** But the wisdom from above is first pure, then peaceable, gentle, open to reason, full of mercy and good

fruits, without uncertainty or insincerity. And the harvest of righteousness is sown in peace by those who make peace." (James 3:5–10, 13–18; all emphases added)

What man is there who desires life,
    and covets many days, that he may enjoy good?
Keep your tongue from evil,
    and your lips from speaking deceit.
Depart from evil, and do good;
    seek peace, and pursue it." (Ps. 34:12–14; emphasis added)
He who speaks the truth gives honest evidence,
    but a false witness utters deceit.
There is one whose rash words are like sword thrusts,
    but the tongue of the wise brings healing.
Truthful lips endure forever,
    but a lying tongue is but for a moment.
Deceit is in the heart of those who devise evil,
    but those who plan good have joy.
. . . .
Lying lips are an abomination to the Lord,
    but those who act faithfully are his delight." (Prov. 12:17–20; 22)

May we pray for the repose of Luther's soul. His troubled life has compromised mankind's religious relationship with God.

REFLECTIONS

1. Which came first: the Church or the Bible?

2. Who gave man the authority to change Sacred Scripture post-Reformation?

3. Did Martin Luther or any other reformer receive or possess divine revelation?

Chapter 4

The Reformation Spreads to the Americas

*For the time is coming when people will **not endure sound teaching**, but having itching ears **they will accumulate for themselves teachers to suit their own likings, and will turn away from listening to the truth and wander into myths**.*
(2 Tim. 4:3–4; all emphases added)

Thus far, we have examined the initial "protest" of Protestantism against the Catholic Church.

Launched in Germany, it was packaged, marketed, and sold as a "reformation" of Jesus' Church to the world. The "Catholic Church" was portrayed as bad and evil, though the state-church was esteemed as good and righteous. Luther self-interpreted Scripture to produce a different theology. Luther's theology was not found in Jesus' Church, nor was it ever taught by the apostles and earliest Church Fathers. Much of his new theology stemmed from one Bible verse, Romans 1:17, as we previously mentioned. He claimed that he was wiser than all historical doctors of the Church. He advocated the killing of German peasants and Jews who did not buy into and convert to his new religion of Christianity, as defined by him. No true Christian advocates violence against humanity, especially God's Chosen, the Jews.

Most importantly, he rejected divine revelation as the foundation of Jesus' Church.

But if a man could do this, why not others? The "new theology" of soteriology broke like an egg, and its yoke would soon ooze over the globe, first within Europe, then on to England, and eventually to the New World.

Volumes could be, and have been, devoted to this topic. But let us continue with a brief study of just two other European men whose quest was simple: follow the Luther Reformation model principles. We use these two men as examples in addition to Luther because from Germany, England, and France, many forms of Protestant religion came to the New World.

Let's pick up where we left off. Luther was enjoying success in establishing Lutheranism (yes, he named his religion after himself) in Germany. He taught that *sola fide* and *sola scriptura* were the only beliefs necessary for salvation, and of course, that one must subscribe to all his teachings. But now John Calvin comes on stage.

John Calvin

Calvin was a French Catholic theologian, lawyer, and humanist who broke away from the Catholic Church. In 1536, he moved from France to Strasburg, Germany. Calvin was learned and greatly studied the Reformation movement in Germany. He was twenty-six years younger than Luther and well-acquainted with the success of the Reformation. He too had studied the Bible. In doing so, he came to envision an entire society governed by the Bible and its teachings, though excluding the Catholic Church. He too utilized a few Bible verses and self-interpreted them to form a new religious theory on salvation. In the conception of his soteriology, as well, there was no divine intervention. None. This would become Calvinism, named again after himself. It too would morph, or splinter, into various branches today — the most well-known being Presbyterianism.

Let us study what drove his personal soteriology. But first, let us remember the immutable words of Sacred Scripture:

> And we have the prophetic word made more sure. You will do well to pay attention to this as to a lamp shining in a dark place, until the day dawns and the morning star rises in your hearts. **First of all you must understand this, that no prophecy of scripture is a matter of one's own interpretation, because no prophecy ever came by the impulse of man,** but men moved by the Holy Spirit spoke from God. (2 Pet. 1:19–21; emphasis added)

Many Protestants would argue that the Holy Spirit must have spoken to or moved Calvin to self-interpret the Bible. However: 1) nowhere in Scripture does it say that other men would come along and have the authority or permission of God to do this, and 2) to establish this as fact, Jesus and the Bible are clear that all facts must be established on the testimony of two or three other witnesses (Moses in Deut. 19:15, Jesus in Matt. 18:16, and Paul in 2 Cor. 13:1 and Heb.10:28). There were no witnesses to such divine intervention.

The Catholic Church teaches that to arrive at what the Bible truly means is to believe as the authors did in their own words. We must know the authors' intentions, not our intentions. To create a religion, one must separate from Jesus' Church. Remember that Calvin too was Roman Catholic. His reason for justifying separation was found in Ephesians 4:11–12, where St. Paul discusses diversity of the gifts of the Spirit after Jesus' Ascension. St. Paul wrote:

> And his [Jesus'] gifts were that some should be apostles, some prophets, some evangelists, some pastors and teachers, for the equipment of the saints, for the work of the ministry, for building up the body of Christ. (Eph. 4:11–12)

Calvin needed his own human authority and not the apostolic Roman Catholic Church's authority. Luther denied the papacy and that authority of the Church. Calvin needed to also claim that his view of Christianity was somehow superior to God and His chosen apostles. So, Calvin claimed that God did call some as apostles, prophets, and evangelists. But somehow, God intended this to be limited in time and temporary until the New Testament was written. So de facto, Christianity somehow was started after the New Testament was created. He would argue that the latter two offices St. Paul mentions that God gave some men were "pastors and teachers." These two offices were to be established on earth and formed by his church structure. Gone were apostolic authority, apostolic succession, and the Roman Catholic Church. Remember, the Bible was constructed by the Roman Catholic Church. Both he and Luther conveniently don't acknowledge their own source, the Roman Catholic Church.

More troubling was Calvin's soteriology on predestination. Here again, he would not only create a new salvation theory but also vigorously defend it. Calvin read the Gospel of John 6:65, which states, "And he [Jesus] said, 'This is why I told you that no one can come to me unless it is granted him by the Father.'" From this one verse, Calvin created another salvation theory — predestination. In its purest form, it theorizes that God, who is eternal and always existed, has predestined people for either salvation or damnation. Period. There is some sort of divine election of one's soul that was predestined before time as God created each of us. When a man takes a Bible verse out of context, a theology is created. If

God only saves the "elect" or a predestined group of people, then some people are guaranteed salvation (eternal life), and everyone else is damned to Hell. Perhaps he failed to read Jesus' own words, "I and the Father are one" (John 10:30), and "The words that I say to you I do not speak on my own authority; but the Father who dwells in me does his works" (John 14:10).

In Calvin's words:

> All are not created on equal terms but some are **preordained** to eternal life, others to eternal damnation; and, accordingly, as each has been created for one or the other of these ends, we say that he has been **predestined** to life or death.[25]

To most of today's Christians, this is insane. How can you be damned by believing in Christ and having faith in Him *and* damned if you don't? In Calvin's view, we have no responsibility for salvation; one's salvation has been predestined by God the Father without one's free will. Scripture clearly states that God wishes all mankind to be saved, future tense.

Like a true ex-Catholic reformer, he described what he considered to be the "true church" along with its ministry, authority, and sacraments. Indeed, he would create his church. Calvin also denied any papal authority and declared all reformers as not schismatic. He argued that the Church was universally "catholic" and therefore concluded and stated, "[The reformers] had to leave them [The Roman Catholic Church] **in order that we might come to Christ**"[26] He

---

[25] Calvin, John. *Institutes of Christian Religion*, bk. 3, chap. 21, par. 5; all emphases added.

[26] T. H. L. Parker, *Calvin: An Introduction to His Thought* (London: Chapman, 1995), p. 134; emphasis added; see Wilhelm Niesel, *The Theology of Calvin* (Grand Rapids, MI: Baker Book House, 1980), pp. 187–195.

would only recognize two sacraments: Baptism and what he relabeled the Lord's Supper.

Calvin's theology was rooted in Geneva, Switzerland, but would spread to France, Germany, Scotland (through John Knox), and the Church of England. He too would use Protestant principles to establish a religious government. Although he preached that the church and the state should not interfere with each other, he propelled himself into religious politics and accepted the position of supreme leader and religious dictator of Geneva, Switzerland, in 1555 and declared it a Protestant city. He was empowered to root out all forms of Catholicism and any immoral activities through the new sumptuary laws he promulgated. These included no swearing, gambling, partying, or dancing. Another state-church.

Henry VIII

To understand the situation of Protestantism in America, we must briefly review what happened in England. King Henry VIII was a staunch Catholic. In fact, when Martin Luther protested the Catholic Church, Henry **initially** repudiated Luther and his arguments. Yet only a decade later, this very same man would unilaterally break from the Catholic Church by establishing himself as the supreme head of the new Church of England. He would seize and dissolve the Catholic monasteries and either absorb or redistribute the property as he deemed. He was, in a sense, the antithesis of St. Paul: Paul went from persecutor of Christ's Church to the greatest evangelical missionary and staunch defender of the Church and its faith. Poor Henry went from a defender of the Church of Jesus to a tyrannical destroyer of the Roman Catholic Church. Why? Human nature and the sinfulness of man.

The Reformation Spreads to the Americas

By 1527, Henry had a problem. His first marriage to Catherine of Aragon had not produced a son or heir. He was smitten by Anne Boleyn, who was one of his wife's ladies-in-waiting. Henry asked Pope Clement VII to grant him a divorce, since Catherine had been previously married to the King's late brother. The pope wouldn't do it. Among other things, granting the divorce would have created a political mess, as King Charles V of Spain was also the emperor of the Holy Roman Empire and the nephew of Catherine of Aragon, Henry's wife. What a drama! So, the king grew impatient and through two Protestant men — clergyman Thomas Cranmer and Thomas Cromwell — a case was made that there was no papal authority over the king and England. Sound familiar? There is a pattern here. Henry was eager to marry Anne; the king appointed Cranmer the archbishop of Canterbury; the archbishop in turn granted Henry his divorce from Catherine. Problem solved.

In 1533, Anne was crowned queen and promptly became pregnant. In 1534, Parliament passed the Act of Supremacy, solidifying the break from the Catholic Church and making King Henry the supreme head of the Church of England. With Cranmer, Cromwell, and Anne, his new wife, all being Protestants, the king quickly followed the Reformation's lessons of destroying the Catholic Church in England. Another state-church was founded. Unfortunately, this one would be more dangerous and brutal because Henry wore two crowns: one as the king and the other as the "king" of the Church of England. Once again, a state-church emerged like Luther's in Germany and Calvin's in Switzerland. Only this time, the king would murder, persecute, and seize the property of anyone in the way of his ambitions.

Between 1536 and 1540, the greatest redistribution of property in England since the Norman Conquest of 1066 would take place. All Catholic property would revert to the king and his crown. Henry would use this property to reward his Protestant counselors for their loyalty. It was Henry's desire for a divorce that caused this mess — and what ensued was a complete tragedy.

Was Henry really the representative of God on earth? He would marry five more times after Catherine, and he had his second and fifth wives executed.

All of the men that Henry chose to lead his newly established Church of England drank from the same chalice of the Protestant Reformation, spreading within a decade from Central Europe. In fact, he and his minions became the vilest of men by committing violence among others who did not subscribe to their church. Estimates vary, but Henry ordered the execution of perhaps up to seventy-two thousand subjects during his reign.

The executions of King Henry VIII are worth study. Many were killed for the state-defined crime of "heresy," the definition of *heresy* often changing depending on Henry's opinion or the person charged. The northern portion of England was a threat to Henry's religious actions. The people protested the religious reforms and the seizing and dissolution of the Catholic monasteries. Henry had them quickly executed. This became known as the Pilgrimage of Grace. Many notable religious were executed by this church king for refusing to acknowledge that he was the supreme leader of the Church. Elizabeth Barton, a nun; Carthusian monks Augustine Webster, Robert Lawrence, and John Houghton; Cardinal St. John Fisher; and St. Thomas More are but a few who would accept martyrdom before declaring Henry as God's chosen successor and denouncing Christ's true Church.

These were the men who shattered Christendom in the sixteenth century in Europe and England. Much more damage would follow.

The very first translation of the Bible into the English language came from within the Roman Catholic Church, when all seventy-three books were translated from Latin to English in 1609. This is known as the Douay-Rheims Bible. But the Protestant Bible had to be different and authorized by the king (man), not the Church.

In 1611, King James I of England authorized the New English Translation of the English Crown's Bible version and ensured that it would be a Protestant Bible (as Luther intended). It had been worked on by reformers for almost a century, but only by Protestants. But as translations multiplied, words changed, and sacred texts were disputed or eliminated, the fracturing of Christendom continued, and spread even to the New World. With these man-made Bibles, men could promulgate their created salvation theories.

The Pilgrims

Many Americans believe that Christianity came to the New World with the pilgrims and the Puritans. This is inaccurate, though it is what most are taught in secular schools. It is true that these two groups came principally from England. However, to understand history properly, we have to go back to the roots of Luther's Protestant Reformation of 1517 and see how it swept across Europe.

In England, every citizen was expected to attend the Church of England. Those who refused were severely punished for treason. Their homes would be confiscated; they would lose their livelihood and face imprisonment or death. Nevertheless, groups of farmers met secretly to worship. They became known as Separatists. They were forced to flee to the Netherlands, which was more tolerant of religious diversity.

After about twelve years there, they began to feel that they were losing their English roots and culture amongst the culture of the Netherlands. They decided to become English Christians (outside the rule of the king's church) and form their colony in the New World. Their spiritual leader, Rev. John Robinson, didn't make the trip. Rather, it was William Bradford who would lead the pilgrims for Delfshaven, where the ship would take the Separatists to transfer to the Mayflower in London for the voyage to the New World.

These Separatists were essentially English Protestants heavily influenced by John Calvin. They did not believe in church hierarchy or in all of the sacraments. They also wished that the Church of England would be purified of its Roman Catholic roots or any of its influence. They were a sect of the Puritan movement. They knew that they were "pilgrims" who would set out for a colony where they could worship (Protestantism) freely. So, they intended to physically separate from the Church of England. They would land in what is modern-day Plymouth, Massachusetts, in November 1620. They were motivated by religious freedom only. No authoritative body would oversee their religious pursuits. They were their own authority.

The Puritan Movement

The Puritans were the larger group of which the pilgrim Separatists were a part. Pilgrim Separatists believed that they had to leave the Church of England completely so that their religious community would be completely separate from the state-church. Most Puritans, however, did not completely abandon the larger Church of England. They thought that they could reform or "purify" the new state-church of England from within. (Note: after one generation, the new state-church of England would be reforming itself already.) In particular, the Puritans would accept the Church of England's ecclesiastical structure, but would operate as congregations in a biblical way, much like the Separatists.

By staying under and somewhat aligned with the Church of England, the Puritans were much wealthier than the pilgrim Separatists. They saw the New World as an investment opportunity in addition to an effort to create "a church that will be a light to the nations," as their leader, John Winthrop, would say. In essence, they thought that by being in a new continent, they could create the purified Church of England.

In 1630, when the Puritans settled in the Massachusetts Bay Colony, they brought money and power. Indeed, they had an official charter from the King of England to establish a British colony. That is one of the reasons why they stayed in the state-church. Within a decade, they would dwarf the pilgrim Separatists. The Puritans would boast about twenty thousand people, while the pilgrims had only about 2,600.

It is a myth to teach that our country was founded on the religious freedom of the pilgrims. They wanted freedom from both Jesus' Church, the Roman Catholic Church, *and* the man-made Church of England. The Puritans demanded separation only from the Catholic Church.

The modern-day religious sects stemming from the Puritans include the current Congregationalist churches, including the Quakers, Unitarians, and Baptists. And indeed, the Puritans arrived in 1620, and their legacy was present when the United States began in 1776. However, the question remains: How and when did Christianity come to the New World?

Catholicism in the New World

Here is the truth as to how Christianity came to the New World. It was brought by the Catholic Church. In 1492, Columbus sailed to find new sea routes for trade to India, China, and the Spice Islands. He had only ninety men on three ships from Spain: the *Nina* (derived from the Latin and Hebrew roots — *Anna*, meaning "Full of Grace"), the *Pinta* ("mark," or "spot"), and the *Santa Maria* ("Holy Mary"). Due to the danger, no priests were allowed to travel on this first voyage.

Columbus's second voyage was in 1493. He had seventeen ships and about 1,200 men. In addition to exploring sea routes, Columbus was a devout, pious man who rigorously practiced the Catholic Faith. Evangelization of the New World was a main priority. On this second voyage, there were five priests among the men: Benedictine Fr. Buil, Hieronymite Fr. Ramon Pane, and three Franciscan friars. The goal of the priests was to evangelize the natives as Christ commanded in the Great Commission.

Columbus died on May 20, 1506, surrounded by fellow Franciscans and his sons. His final words were those of Christ Himself, "Into your hands, O Lord, I commend my spirit" (see Luke 23:46). This is when the good news arrived in the New World, some 127 years earlier than the date taught to American students today.

The Spanish explorers and missionary evangelists had a difficult time converting the natives to Christianity. The power and brutality of human sacrifice practiced by the Aztecs stood in their way. It would take Cortez and the Conquistadors to finally suppress human sacrifice. Not until 1521 did a full-scale conversion to Christianity begin. The mendicant orders of Franciscans, Dominicans, and Augustinians were sent to the New World, called New Spain, to convert all indigenous peoples. Initially, in 1524, twelve Franciscans would arrive to help convert New Spain to Christianity. In 1526, the Dominican Order would arrive, and finally, in 1533, the Augustinians. Many Roman Catholic Churches were built immediately.

During these times, Our Blessed Mother appeared as Our Lady of Guadalupe to a humble native who is now a saint, Juan Diego. These apparitions occurred in 1531 at Tepeyac Hill, modern-day Mexico City. What makes this Marian apparition distinct from her other Church-approved apparitions is that Mary appeared in her glorified body, and her actual hands rearranged roses in Juan Diego's *tilma*. A *tilma* was the native's outer cloak garment made of cactus fibers, which deteriorate and fall apart within fifteen to twenty years. St. Juan Diego's *tilma*, which is intact, is on display at the Basilica of Our Lady of Guadalupe. Many miracles and interventions are attributed to Our Lady of Guadalupe. To this day, the basilica is the one of most visited Christian sites on the planet, with some twenty million people annually making a pilgrimage there to witness the *tilma* and learn the Christian message: evangelize and build churches in Jesus' Name.

Multiplication of Churches

Though Catholicism came first to the New World, Protestantism flourished in North America thanks to the Puritans. But the sheer number of churches that we see today is the legacy of Martin Luther and the Protestant belief in self-interpretation or private interpretation of the Bible.

But didn't Our Lord say, "There shall be **one flock, one shepherd** [emphasis added]" (John 10:16)? Yet various Christian denominations cannot agree on what Christ taught. Christ condemned denominationalism when He stated, "And if a house is divided against itself, that house will not be able to stand" (Mark 3:25). Remember that the Church is "the household of God" (1 Tim. 3:15). Catholic Christians wouldn't believe that Christ would ever sanction division in His Church based upon the clear teaching of Scripture. All the Christian sects are called "Protestants" because they all unite in one objective: protesting their mother, the Roman Catholic Church.

Today, there are many different Protestant churches because there are now so many interpretations of the Bible. There are so many different interpretations of the Bible because there are so many wrong interpretations of the Bible, and there are so many wrong interpretations because the system of interpreting the Bible is radically wrong. It is self-interpretation! We cannot have *one* fold, *one* shepherd, *one* Faith, and *one* Baptism of Christianity if every man and woman interprets Sacred Scripture according to their pet theories, emotional needs, or humanist theology.

There is no whim, fad, or fancy that someone does not claim to prove from the Bible. Virtually any literate person can claim the role of a competent interpreter of the Word of God. Somehow, these people believe that God abandoned this world from 1500–1900 (four hundred years) and that the Christian world of Christendom was in total darkness. They also profess that by them alone light has finally come into the world. What a mess this has made. Here are but a few examples of the fruit of man's tinkering with God's Church:

> Some of these modern sects, just like the early heretics, will "prove" from the Bible that in the New Law Christ is only God and not man. Others, like modern Unitarians, will "prove" to you from the Bible that Christ is only man and not God.
>
> Campbellites will "prove" from the Bible that Baptism is unnecessary for children and necessary for adults only. Others will "prove" from the Bible that the whole of Baptism is a ceremony, an initiation like joining a lodge. By the same Word, some believe it only cleanses from Original Sin while others believe it forgives all sins and that salvation is somehow guaranteed. Then there is the method of Baptism. Some will teach from the Bible that one must be immersed in water while others will "prove" to you from the Bible that the entire baptismal process is a superstition and should be abandoned.

The Reformation Spreads to the Americas

Some denominations argue from the Bible that in the New Law, Christ shared His priesthood with no one. Others can simultaneously "prove" to you from the Bible that in the New Law, even women are now priests; hence "presbyters" or "priests," from which the "Presbyterian" sect is found.

Fanatical groups "prove" from the Bible that there is going to be a millennium, a thousand years when everyone will somehow get a second trial or chance. Meanwhile, as we have discussed, Calvinists will "prove" to you from the Bible that a large part of mankind does not even get a first trial but is simply predestined to damnation irrespective of one's merits or Jesus' mercy.

Some people "prove" by the Bible that eternal punishment is going to be meted out to nearly everyone; and that somehow God will take care of a little handful of a particular sect. This is spiritual blackmail! Still others will "prove" from the Bible the exact opposite — that everyone will be saved. Do *you* believe that even to unrepentant murderers, adulterers, robbers of widows and orphans, and sodomites Christ will hold out His arms and say, "Come, O blessed of my Father, inherit the kingdom prepared for you from the foundation of the world" (Matt. 25:34)?

Many Protestant denominations will "prove" from the Bible that it is faith alone that gets you to Heaven and works do not matter at all. Meanwhile, Mormonism, a splinter Protestant sect from the 1820s, will "prove" from their Bible that works are all that matters.

When you reduce it to practice, the Protestant theory foundationally means this: read the Bible and believe what you like. If you like Martin

Luther's theory, follow it; if you prefer Calvin's Christianity, embrace it; if you think Thomas Campbell, Joseph Smith, Mrs. Eddy, or Pastor Russell have somehow "discovered" the truth and thus have now succeeded in doing what Christ Himself must have failed to do, then take them as your guide. And if one of these theories fails to suit you, either make one up yourself or wait until next week, as there will be another church on the corner.

Some more recent fallacies include Mrs. Mary Baker Eddy, the founder of the Church of Jesus Christ Scientist, also known simply as Christian Science (1879). She "proved" from the Bible that man is all soul, where the body is practically a delusion and does not exist. There are "Bible students" who will "prove" from the Bible that the soul is all a delusion — you do not have one. When you die, you do not know anything; the soul which God gave Adam was only air and nothing else. Also, we read in the Bible to "serve the Lord with fear, and trembling" (Ps. 2:11), so there are the Christians who call themselves the shakers and the weepers. Again, in the Bible we are told to "rejoice in the Lord always; again I will say, Rejoice" (Phil. 4:4). And thus, we have the jumpers, the snake handlers, the holy laughers, and roller Christians. You would think that by now that there would be sufficient variety to accommodate everyone's beliefs. But new sects continue to spring up.

In essence, what they are all saying is this: "Christ's Church for two thousand years was a complete failure, but fortunately for the world, a man has come to finally set it right."

We started this chapter with a quote from St. Paul concerning his prophecy that in time people will not tolerate sound doctrine; but through their desires and curiosities, they will acquire an increasing number of teachers. St. Paul also warned us that through human volition, people will stop listening to the truth and be sidetracked into fallacy or myths. St. Peter emphasizes what St. Paul meant when he wrote:

> So also our beloved brother Paul wrote to you according to the wisdom given him, speaking of this as he does in all his letters. There are some things in them hard to understand, which the ignorant and the unstable **twist to their own destruction, as they do the other scriptures.**" (2 Pet. 3:15–16; emphasis added)

For anyone who wishes to understand where they "sit" relative to Christianity, this graph will help. It depicts the branching or splintering of Protestantism from the Reformation to today. If the reader is Protestant, they should note that where they are today in their individual Christian journey has its root from Henry VIII, Martin Luther, John Calvin, or another historical figure. If you don't find your church in this diagram, simply ask your pastor where he learned his Christian teachings and it will become apparent which "box" you fall into — or to which box you should connect your new box.

ONE LORD, ONE FAITH, ONE CHURCH

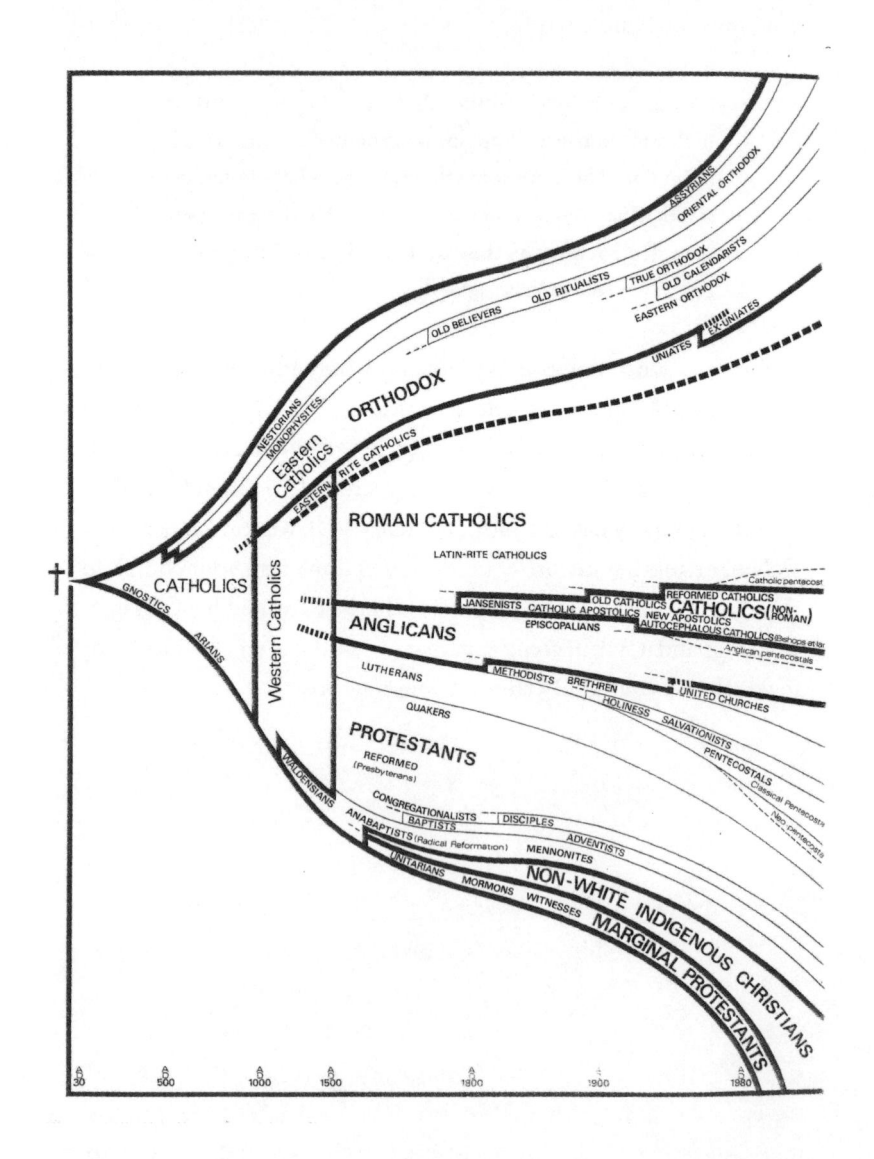

CATHOLICS

GNOSTICS
ARIANS

Eastern Catholics
NESTORIANS
MONOPHYSITES
EASTERN-RITE CATHOLICS

ORTHODOX
ASSYRIANS
ORIENTAL ORTHODOX
OLD RITUALISTS
TRUE ORTHODOX
OLD CALENDARISTS
OLD BELIEVERS
EASTERN ORTHODOX
UNIATES
EX-UNIATES

Western Catholics

ROMAN CATHOLICS
LATIN-RITE CATHOLICS
JANSENISTS
OLD CATHOLICS
CATHOLIC APOSTOLICS
REFORMED CATHOLICS
NEW APOSTOLICS
CATHOLICS (NON-ROMAN)
AUTOCEPHALOUS CATHOLICS
Catholic pentecostals
Bishops at large

ANGLICANS
EPISCOPALIANS
Anglican pentecostals

PROTESTANTS
LUTHERANS
METHODISTS
BRETHREN
HOLINESS
SALVATIONISTS
UNITED CHURCHES
QUAKERS
PENTECOSTALS
Classical Pentecostals
Neo-Pentecostals
REFORMED (Presbyterians)
CONGREGATIONALISTS
BAPTISTS
DISCIPLES
ADVENTISTS
ANABAPTISTS (Radical Reformation)
MENNONITES

NON-WHITE INDIGENOUS CHRISTIANS

MARGINAL PROTESTANTS
UNITARIANS
MORMONS
WITNESSES

AD 30 | AD 500 | AD 1000 | AD 1500 | AD 1800 | AD 1900 | AD 1980

False Teachings

Scripture is laden with the warnings of false teachers, especially within the Church herself. St. Paul was best at telling us about a gospel message that was contrary to the apostles' gospel message. He said, "But even **if we, or an angel from heaven, should preach to you a gospel contrary to that which we preached to you, let him be accursed**" (Gal. 1:8; emphasis added). The vast majority of Christians would, we surmise, agree with St. Paul's statement. But they can't all agree on what he means.

Here is an example. Suppose that there are ten people and they all profess to be Christians. Now give them all the same basic arithmetic problem. What is two plus two? There is only *one true* answer and millions of wrong answers. Now suppose you take these same ten people and ask them, "What does the Bible teach about salvation?" If they are not Catholic, you will most likely get ten different answers. Now multiply ten times hundreds of millions of people — well, you get the point. There will be thousands upon thousands of differing answers.

All this disorder and lack of unity started in the Reformation and is rapidly progressing. Once humans alone can "self-interpret" the Bible, realistically, we have eight billion differing beliefs. One for every man, woman, and child. In that process, truth is relative to human thought, which is always limited, finite, and human only. Every Christian religious sect or church started by a mortal man (other than the Church Jesus started, which is the Catholic Church), embraces the tenets of Protestantism: 1) reject the authority of Christ's established Catholic Church; 2) refuse to accept the office of the papacy established with Peter and apostolic succession; 3) refuse to accept the seven sacraments of Christ's Church; and 4) refuse to accept all teachings and doctrine of His holy Church which have been handed down by Christ and His apostolic Church for over two thousand years.

But just because you think something or were told by another mortal to believe something does *not* make it true. If God and Christ are Truth and the Holy Spirit leads us to Truth, then one should seek God's Truth. As we previously mentioned, St. Augustine explains how he came to faith in Jesus Christ, "I would not believe the gospel myself if the authority of the Catholic Church did not move me to do so."

The Church's Authority

Let us use another example from Scripture to enlighten the reader concerning the point of Church authority as established by Jesus Himself. The Gospel of John has the longest record of the events of the Last Supper, in chapters 13 through 17. This section is known in the Catholic Church as "The Book of Glory." In fact, this is so relevant, that St. John devotes approximately 25 percent of his entire Gospel message about this one event of Jesus' life at the Last Supper. In Christ's thirty-three earthly years, St. John devotes approximately one-fourth of his Gospel to one evening in the life of Jesus Christ. Surely Our Lord must have chosen His words carefully when He spoke to the apostles about His Passion. Chapter 17 is comprised only of the spoken words of Our Lord. No other person is recorded in the transcript. In the Bible, Jesus often prayed alone, in solitude, and on a mountain. Here we finally get a glimpse of God the Son praying to God the Father recorded for all to read. The eleven apostles simply listened — Judas has fled. Jesus' final prayer was to his Father, our Father — God. Some very important events happened here, but we must pay attention to the words themselves. Jesus' words matter. He was speaking **only** to the apostles who were chosen by Him to build His Church on earth once He resurrected and ascended to Heaven:

When Jesus had spoken these words, he lifted up his eyes to heaven and said, "Father, the hour has come [the hour of His Passion and immolation]; glorify thy Son that the Son may glorify thee, since thou hast given him power over all flesh, to give eternal life to all whom thou hast given him. And this is eternal life, that ***they* know thee the only true God, and Jesus Christ whom thou hast sent.** I glorified thee on earth, having accomplished the work which thou gavest me to do; and now, Father, glorify thou me in thy own presence with the glory which I had with thee **before the world was made** [Jesus preexisted all time and space]. I have manifested thy name to **the men whom thou gavest me out of the world** [**the eleven apostles in His presence**]; ***thine they*** [**the eleven apostles**] ***were*, and thou [*God*] gavest *them* to me, and *they*** [**the eleven apostles**] **have kept thy word.** Now *they* know that everything that thou hast given me is from thee; for I have given *them* the words which thou gavest me, and *they* have received them and know in truth that I came from thee; and *they* have believed that thou didst send me. **I am praying for *them*; I am not praying for the world but for those whom thou hast given me, for they are thine; all mine are thine, and thine are mine, and I am glorified in *them*** [all emphases added]." (John 17:1–10)

Note that Jesus was praying to God the Father and thanks Him for choosing these men, the eleven apostles. Simply notice the "they" and "them" references. Any other person cannot superimpose himself or herself into these verses, yet many do.

Let's continue in John 17:

And now I am no more in the world, but they are in the world, and I am coming to thee. Holy Father, keep ***them***

> [**the eleven apostles**] in thy name, which thou hast given me, that they may be one, even as we are one. [Jesus prays that all the apostles are to be as *one*; as He and God the Father are *one*; unity in purpose, doctrine, and faith.] While I was with ***them*, I kept *them*** [**the eleven apostles**] in thy name, which thou hast given me; I have guarded ***them***, and none of ***them*** is lost but the son of perdition, that the scripture might be fulfilled. (John 17:11–12; all emphases added)

It is clear that Jesus was ***only speaking*** to and about the apostles in his reference to ***them***; for he made the exception referencing Judas, called the "son of perdition," who was not amongst the eleven. Jesus' prayer continued:

> But now I am coming to thee; and these things I speak in the world; that ***they*** may have my joy fulfilled in ***themselves***. I have given ***them*** **thy word;** and the world has hated ***them*** because ***they*** are not of the world, even as I am not of the world. I do not pray that thou shouldst take ***them*** out of the world, but that thou shouldst keep ***them*** from the evil one. ***They*** are not of the world, even as I am not of the world." (John 17:13–16; all emphases added)

Jesus was stating that both He and the apostles are not of this earthly world. He also noted that this world would hate them and that the Father would protect them from the evil one:

> **Sanctify *them* in the truth; thy word is *truth*. As thou didst send *me* into the world, so I have sent *them* (the eleven apostles) into the world. And for *their* sake I consecrate myself, that *they* (the eleven apostles) also**

may be *consecrated in truth.*" (John 17:17–19; emphasis added)

Jesus performed a bilateral consecration here. God's Word is Truth, and Jesus asked that the apostles be consecrated in God the Father, who is Truth. Then Christ consecrated Himself into them. God's Word is Truth, Jesus is Truth, and the eleven apostles were consecrated by Jesus personally. To consecrate means to declare and make one holy for a divine purpose. These men were now dedicated to a sacred use by God and Jesus. It also means to ordain to a sacred office. When Jesus asked for them to be sanctified, this too meant to be made holy as a vessel full of the Holy Spirit.

These are the only men in the history of humanity made holy by Jesus' prayer of consecration to God, the Father. His prayer continued and moved from the present to the future concerning disciples who would come to know Jesus for their eternal salvation. This means you and me and all our loved ones. The future believers in Christ. Now that their consecration had occurred by Jesus Himself, Jesus spoke to those who would come to believe in Him by saying the following as He continued His prayer to God, the Father: "I do not pray for these only, but also for those who believe in me **through their [the eleven apostles'] word**, that they may all be one; even as thou, Father, art in me, and I in thee, that they also may be in us, so that the world may believe that thou hast sent me" (John 17:20–21; emphasis added).

These verses spoke to future disciples of Christ and His Church. He demanded unity in His Church. There was no disunity spoken about. He also was very direct in His petitions to God the Father in that all future human generations are to come to believe that God sent Jesus to redeem mankind. He clearly stated that all future generations are to come to this belief (meaning faith) through only the words of the apostles and His Church; for He Himself said so. Jesus further expounded: "The glory which thou hast given me I have given **them**, that they may be one even as we are one, **I in *them* and thou in me, that *they*** may become perfectly one, so that the world may know that **thou hast sent me and hast loved *them* even as thou hast loved me**. Father, I desire that ***they*** also, whom thou hast given me, may be with me where I am, to behold my glory which thou hast given me in thy love for me before the foundation of the world" (John 17:22–24; all emphases added).

Notice the past tense in that Jesus has *"given"* them. Meaning only this message of unity in purpose and truth was given to the apostles and their successors. These men would in fact "see Jesus' glory," namely, His death, Resurrection, and subsequent Ascension. Jesus concluded His prayer to God the Father: "O righteous Father, the world has not known thee, but I have known thee; and ***these*** know that thou hast sent me. I made known to ***them*** **thy name, and I will make it known, that the love with which thou hast loved me may be in *them*, and I in *them*"** (John 17:25–26; all emphases added). Jesus concluded His prayer for the apostles who will build His Church by asking God the Father to place the love between the Father and the Son in them. Jesus' last statement was that He is in *them*!

This is the apostolic charter. The final instructions to and for the group of eleven men hand-chosen by Christ during His earthly ministry to establish His one, holy, catholic, and apostolic Church before His Passion and death on the Cross. Peter was chosen by God Himself as their leader. This helped to ensure unity, for if there were eleven co-equal leaders, human nature would yield division. Jesus knew that He was going to depart this earth as His purpose was almost complete. He knew the Father's will and He actively sought this in His life to perfection. He was born to die.

The Last Supper was truly Christ Himself, the foundation stone of His Church, praying to God the Father for the oneness of His Church. The consecrations and command from Our Lord that all are to come to faith through **their words** is irrefutable. The eleven apostles never fragmented the message and teachings of Jesus and His Church, nor did St. Paul, nor did the seventy-two hand-selected by Christ (most became bishops of the Church), nor did the successors. One Body of Christ, one Christendom, one Church. This was always God's plan. This one Church would produce the Bible. Even in the days of the apostles and thereafter, men arose within the Church as heretics. This is nothing new. The Church has dealt with all heresies to date and will continue to do so. We know by Christ's own words that the gates of Hell will not prevail against His Church.

We have now learned how the seeds of Protestantism, or the Reformation, were planted by various men and women — many of whom were originally of and within Jesus' Church. Humans have history, and we operate inside of time. God does not. (Evidently, He states, "For I the Lord do not change," Mal. 3:6; and "Jesus Christ is the same yesterday and today and for ever," Heb. 13:8.) Why then would mankind embark on folly and dare to start new Christian faiths and sects by altering the beliefs and teachings of Christ's Church? The answer lies in the Fall itself.

Man loves to reject the authority of Christ's Mystical Body, His Church. Christ told the apostles and His Church to not be of this world. Human beings are constantly plagued with the dilemma of moral principles, hence the seven cardinal sins, or vices, that work against the seven cardinal virtues of humans. These seven deadly vices are pride, greed, wrath, envy, lust, gluttony, and sloth. When one studies man's motivations to establish religions or churches, normally one can find one or more of the vices cloaked under the guise of being "godly." If you would like more detail on these, we suggest studying Tertullian, known as a theologian and apologist of Christianity. Tertullian would teach St. Cyprian, who was the predecessor of St. Augustine. Both of these saints are Church Fathers and served as bishops of the Church. And if you want to learn a lot more about what the Catholic Church teaches, you should read the Catholic *Catechism*.

We close this chapter in human history with another quote from St. Augustine, Bishop of Hippo, Church Father and Doctor of the Church:

> If you believe what you like in the Gospel and reject what you do not like, it is not the Gospel you believe, but yourself.[27]

---

[27] William A. Jurgens, *The Faith of the Early Fathers* vol. 3 (Collegeville: Liturgical Press, 1970), 58.

REFLECTIONS

1. Where did God or the Bible ever command a human being to create theology, a religion, or a church?

2. What soteriology (salvation theology) does your pastor or church teach? Is it consistent with Christ's Church's teaching?

3. If you are not Catholic, what branch of the Protestant Reformation tree is your faith seeded from?

CHAPTER 5

DEFINING THE TERM *CHURCH* IN THE UNITED STATES OF AMERICA

Beloved, do not believe every spirit, but test the spirits to see whether they are of God; for many false prophets have gone out into the world.... Little children, you are of God, and have overcome them [the spirits of the world]; for he who is in you is greater than he who is in the world. They are of the world, and the world listens to them. **We are of God. Whoever knows God listens to us [the apostolic Church], and he who is not of God does not listen to us.** *By this we know the spirit of truth and the spirit of error. (1 John 4:1, 4–6; emphasis added)*

IN THE GRAPH OF the chief branches of American Protestant churches presented in chapter 4, you may have recognized your denomination, or that of family members, friends, or neighbors. If your beliefs have led you to a stand-alone independent assembly as a part of a non-denominational church, then you are often referred to as an "Evangelical." Independent Evangelical churches are rapidly growing in the United States and are the direct descendants of former Protestant churches. The splintering or fragmentation of the Reformation continues today. In fact, it is rapidly accelerating.

This phenomenon is readily visible principally in the United States — and we will study why it is accelerating especially from the twentieth century to the current twenty-first century. We will also study factual proof as to why the Roman Catholic Church is the original, and only, Church that Jesus Himself founded upon Himself.

We have studied why the historical fracturing from Christ's holy and apostolic Church occurred along with its causality and timing. We have also studied which key human beings caused the breaking away and how this has led to churches coming to the New World. Now we will examine the United States in particular.

Although we know that Christians cannot all agree on basic theology, doctrine, and the meaning of Scripture, to help clarify our discussion, let us begin this section with simple, uncontroversial definitions from Dictionary.com, whose sources are Random House Unabridged Dictionary, Collins English Dictionary, and American Heritage Dictionary:

Protestant

noun
2. an adherent of any of those Christian bodies that separated from the Church of Rome during the Reformation, or of any group descended from them, usually excluding the Anabaptists.
4. **protestant, a person who protests**. (emphasis added)

adjective
5. belonging or related to Protestants or their religion.

The word *Protestant* was coined by the Lutherans at the Diet of Speyer in 1529.

Protestantism

noun
1. the religion of Protestants.
2. the Protestant churches collectively.

Thus, Protestantism is a branch of Christianity originating in the sixteenth-century Reformation. It is characterized by its doctrines of justification by grace through faith, the priesthood of all believers, and the authority of only Holy Scripture as defined by the reformers.

Evangelical

adjective
2. belonging to or designating the Christian churches that emphasize the teachings and authority of the Scriptures, especially of the New Testament, in **opposition to the institutional authority of the church itself,** and that stress as paramount the tenet that salvation is achieved by personal conversion to faith in the atonement of Christ. (emphasis added)
3. designating Christians, especially of the late 1970s, eschewing the designation of fundamentalist but holding a conservative interpretation of the Bible.
4. pertaining to certain movements in the Protestant churches in the 18th and 19th centuries that stressed the importance of personal experience of guilt for sin, and of reconciliation to God through Christ.

Catholic Church

noun
1. a visible society of baptized Christians **professing the same faith under the authority of the invisible head (Christ) and the authority of the visible**

head (the pope or the bishops in communion with him). (all emphases added)

Heresy

noun
3. The willful and persistent rejection of any article of faith by a baptized member of the church.

With those definitions in mind, let us again consider why the proliferation of churches occurred in the United States.

First, the United States is a country of freedom, which includes the freedom to practice religion. Why not have thousands of religions, which in turn must have thousands of churches to support their congregations in worship and economics? This led to the splintering and forming of new religions becoming normative in the United States. Furthermore, once "faith alone" and self-interpretation of Scripture were emphasized, varying belief systems emerged mostly from select passages of the Bible, systems which then emphasized a particular viewpoint, or at the very least created a new definition of the pathway to salvation and man's practice of worship. An example of this includes the Fundamentalist movements that spawned churches that professed to have a corner on the market of "truth" and vehemently preached intolerance of any other Christian viewpoint and practice. Today in the United States, these are the Assemblies of God, the Southern Baptist Convention, and the Seventh-day Adventists.

Secondly, our own U.S. government has enabled the proliferation of churches by *not* defining the word *church*. This was like throwing gasoline on a fire: a multiplier of denominations, sects, religions, and so-called "Christianity" in its broadest terminology. Our U.S. Treasury Department and Internal Revenue Service (IRS) Code

Defining the Term Church *in the United States of America*

have only ignited the spark that Luther created in the sixteenth century to divide Christendom, shatter the Church, and cause further fragmentation (disunity) of churches. To this day, Congress and the Courts have not defined the words "church", "religion," nor "worship" so as to not run afoul of the First Amendment of the Constitution; freedom of religion and speech.

Remember that Christendom is the political expression of a **Who**: the Church was founded by a living God and the personage of His Son, Our Lord Jesus Christ. If you were a member of the Catholic Church, you belonged to Christ's Body that He established Himself. But the U.S. government would define the word *church* as a **What**. It all started with basic definitions as enacted by the state. The IRS intervened and established the key definitions of the types of entities that are defined as "churches." We compromised on legal (human) definitions for the sake of our tax code. In essence, the IRS needed to define a classification of persons or entities for U.S. tax purposes only. Yes, it is that simple. It was about tax revenue and what legal entities constituted churches to be exempt from taxation. The entity "church" became a state-sponsored **What**.

Whenever nations or countries attempt to define a spiritual institution established by Christ as a legal organization that exists in human time, unintended consequences occur, for example, the continued disunity and nullification of one Christendom. In fact, now any American citizen can start his or her "church." Yes, this is factual. Let us look at this in more detail.

From the IRS website:

> The term **church** is found, ***but not specifically defined,*** **in the Internal Revenue Code**. With the exception of the special rules for church audits, the use of the word **church**

also includes conventions and associations of churches as well as integrated auxiliaries of a church.

Certain characteristics are generally attributed to churches. These attributes of a church have been developed by the IRS and by court decisions. They include:

- Distinct legal existence
- Recognized creed and form of worship
- Definite and distinct ecclesiastical government
- Formal code of doctrine and discipline
- Distinct religious history
- Membership **not** associated with any other church or denomination
- Organization of ordained ministers
- Ordained ministers selected after completing prescribed courses of study
- Literature of its own
- Established places of worship
- Regular congregations
- Regular religious services
- Sunday schools for the religious instructions of the young
- Schools for the preparation of its members

The IRS generally uses a combination of these characteristics, together with other facts and circumstances, to determine whether and organization is considered a **church** for federal tax purposes. Note criteria include "literature of its own" and its members "cannot be associated with any other church or denomination". Now one can understand why there are tens of thousands of churches in the United States.[28]

No single characteristic determines the answer if the IRS will approve your application as not all factors above must be present. Every church application is considered on a case-by-case basis.

The term *church* pertains to meeting or not meeting a "definition" for federal tax purposes. It is a ***What*. A tax-exempt organization is a state-sponsored legal entity.** Notice how a characteristic of a non-defined church is "**membership not associated with any other church or denomination**"; therefore, any U.S. citizen can start a church and seek the required tax-exempt status from the IRS. Yes, you are reading this correctly. Anyone can legally form or start a "church" organization, even though the word is not defined anywhere by the IRS. Legal organizations began proliferating in the United States as tax-exempt churches. Tax exemption is extremely important to achieve. Why? Because for U.S. tax law, churches are "public charities," or 501(c)(3) organizations, as defined by the government. Earning this classification means that they are generally *exempt* from federal, state, and local income and property taxes. "Exempt" means that they do not pay any taxes even though they may collect substantial amounts of money as revenues.

Do you know a church when you see one? Probably not. This is because the IRS has never defined the term. Since there is no standard operating definition, it is automatically subjective. Exactly what constitutes a church for the tax code? Generally, the IRS has come down on this by calling a church a "**place of worship by any religion.**" Yes,

[28] "'Churches' Defined," IRS, accessed April 2, 2024, https://www.irs.gov/charities-non-profits/churches-religious-organizations/churches-defined; emphases added.

you read it correctly. Now the organization doesn't even need to call itself a church! It can call itself a mosque, temple, synagogue, and the like. So broad is the interpretation of the word *church* that the IRS has granted tax-exempt status to the Satanic Temple as a church in the United States. This raises a broader and more difficult question. What constitutes a **religion**? Well, the IRS has decided that it is any group that comes together for worship. There are no black-and-white rules or criteria. The IRS simply wants to know that the organization is not operating for profit, its sole purpose is to worship and make community connections, and that it is not a political organization. This is true but silly. The word *church* is not defined; sadly, neither are the words *worship* or *religion*.

Obtaining a tax-exempt status as a church organization (assuming that one has done the legal entity formation) is as easy as going online with the IRS and applying for a church tax ID number from the IRS. Once the IRS gives you a number, you are a "church" regardless of your so-called "religion." All types of church tax ID or employer identification numbers can be obtained online in about one hour.

Once approved as a church, any subsequent challenges to whether an organization is a "church" are left to the tax court and their rulings.[29] In one case, Chapman v. Commissioner, 48 T.C. 358 (1967), the concept of a "congregation" would emerge to help define *church* for tax purposes. The judges came up with this because even they could not agree on the definition of *church*. Three pseudo-definitions emerged:

---

[29] For an in-depth understanding of the history of the term *church* in the tax code, refer to Charles M. Whalen, " 'Church' in the Internal Revenue Code: The Definitional Problems," *Fordham L. Rev.* 885 (1977): p. 45. Also, Congressional Research Services report IF 12520

1. The term **church** is intended to be synonymous with the terms "denomination" or "sect" rather than to be used universally. [Note to reader — per our government — no universality! Only division.]

2. The word "**church**" implies that an otherwise qualified organization **bring people together as the principle (*sic*) means** of accomplishing its [tax-] exempt purpose. The objects of such gatherings need **not be for the conversion to a particular faith or segment of a faith** nor the propagation of the views of a particular denomination or sect. [Again, the reader should note that the government is promulgating plurality of religions and belief systems, which is contrary to Jesus' command for unity and one flock, one shepherd.]

3. To be a "**church**" a religious organization must engage in the administration of sacerdotal functions and the conduct of religious worship in accordance with the tenets and practices of a particular religious body.[30]

Once again, we are left with no definition of the word *church*. The courts discuss congregations, worship, and religion but have also not defined those terms.

Here are the points to understand: 1) there *is no* mention of God nor His only begotten Son, Our Lord Jesus Christ, relative to anything concerning the word or term *church*; 2) anyone can create

---

[30] Quoted in Robert Louthian and Thomas Miller, "Defining 'Church' — The Concept of a Congregation," appendix D-1 in *Charity Oversight and Reform: Keeping Bad Things from Happening to Good Charities: Hearing before the Committee on Finance, United States Senate,One Hundred Eighth Congress, Second Session, June 22, 2004* (Washington: U.S. Government Printing Office, 2004), p. 340; emphases added.

another branch of so-called "Christianity," much like Luther did because of this enabling state-church-sponsoring tax code; 3) "churches," according to the U.S. government, are organized to "bring people together as the ... means of accomplishing its exempt purpose" of which the objectives "need *not* be the conversion to a particular faith or segment of a faith nor the propagation of the views of a particular denomination or sect" (emphasis added); and 4) this is the equivalent of open borders for any faith, any denomination, any teachings, any worship, or any sect. So much for the Great Commission of Jesus to the apostles.

The Christendom of the world pre-1517 is a distant memory. Many preach unity but do not practice it. In the United States, additional "churches" will only exacerbate division. Why? Because they are "whats," organizations that must survive economically to pay their pastors and staff.

Non-denominational churches have begun to practice survival of the fittest. Many start and many fail. The mega non-denominational churches principally preach a "prosperity gospel," an emotional calling card to those seeking encouragement in our world today. We are sure that many people with good intentions in the United States today truly love Jesus and want nothing more than to establish a personal relationship with Him. This is laudable. Many men and women who have started Christian churches over the past fifty to eighty years in the United States via the U.S. tax code are faithful Christians who most likely believe that this is what God wants them to do. Many of these folks are educated and trained in theology.

The question is: Where in the Bible is the verse or verses that give anyone the authority to start their own "church"?

We have many friends and family members who choose to attend non-denominational churches. The primary attractions are the

Defining the Term Church in the United States of America

pastor (personal relationship), the message preached (someone's interpretation of the Bible that they can either emotionally connect with or rationally agree with), and the people (often like-minded). What we have witnessed is that if any of these three considerations change, people often move to a different church. For example, if the pastor dies or retires and the new successor doesn't fulfill the needs of the person, they tend to "pastor shop." But although this impulse provides freedom and fluidity to seek what one is trying to find, it highlights that what is sought is a human person or experience rather than God Himself.

Sometimes, there is a very dynamic leader in the church and he or she starts their own church, in which case the person leaves to follow a particular charismatic personality — if they don't, very often the message changes when the leaders change. When the message changes because the new person has his own ideas and interpretations of Scripture, the congregant begins searching anew again. Sometimes the choice of a church is simply driven by neighborhood convenience regardless of denomination.

Many faithful Christians are not currently Catholic. However, as we like to say; they are Catholic; they just don't know it yet. In fact, Pope Pius XII says, "By baptism they are incorporated into the Mystical Body of Christ."

One of everyone's favorite evangelists is the late Billy Graham. He and (Pope) St. John Paul II had a wonderful, collegial working relationship. In fact, Billy Graham was preaching in Krakow, Poland, the very day that its native son, Cardinal Archbishop Karol Wojtyla, was elected pope in Rome in 1978. A reporter once asked Mr. Graham what he would do if he were asked to preach at St. Peter's in Rome. His response was, "I would gladly and humbly accept ... [and] study for about a year in preparing."

Did Jesus Want There to Be Many Churches?

We keep coming back to the same question: Did Jesus Christ Himself really want thousands of churches? Was His divine hand involved in the creation of any of these churches? There is no biblical evidence for either of these questions being answered in the affirmative. God established two divinely appointed religions: Old Testament Judaism, which is obsolete (see Heb. 8:13), and New Testament Catholic Christianity, which is eternal (see Heb. 13:20).

Let's look at what normative and standard literature states about Jesus' Church along with some authoritative human witnesses.

From ***The Encyclopedia of Religion***:

> Catholicism does begin at the beginning, that is, with Jesus' gathering of his disciples and with his eventual commissioning ... of Peter to be the chief Shepherd and foundation of the church. Therefore, it is not Roman primacy that gives Catholicism its distinctive identity within the community of Christian churches but the Petrine primacy. Peter is listed first among the twelve and is frequently their spokesperson ... there is increasing agreement that he did go to Rome and was martyred there ... the conferral of the power of the keys (to Peter) clearly suggests an imposing measure of authority, given the symbolism of the keys as instruments for opening and shutting the gates of the kingdom of heaven ... there seems to be a trajectory of images relating to Peter and his ministry that sets him apart within the original company of disciples and explains his ascendancy and that of his successors throughout the early history of the church. Peter is portrayed as the fisherman ... as an elder who addresses other elders, as proclaimer of faith in Jesus ... as

receiver of a special revelation, as one who can correct others for doctrinal matters (2 Pt 3:15–16), and as the rock on which the church is built (Mt 16:18) ... the church adopted the organizational grid of the Roman Empire: localities, dioceses, provinces. It also identified its own center with that of the empire, Rome. Moreover, there was attached to this city (Rome) the tradition that Peter and Paul had founded the church there and that he and Paul were martyred and buried there ... During the first 5 centuries, the Church of Rome gradually assumed preeminence among all the churches. It (the Church in Rome) intervened in the life of the distant churches, took sides in theological controversies, was consulted by other bishops on doctrinal and moral questions, and sent delegates to distant councils. The see of Rome came to be regarded as a kind of final court of appeal as well as a focus of unity for the worldwide communion of churches. The correlation between Peter and the bishop of Rome became fully explicit during the Pontificate of Leo I (A.D. 460–461), who claimed that Peter continued to speak to the whole church through the bishop of Rome.[31]

From ***Encyclopedia Britannica***, under "Roman Catholicism":

[Roman Catholicism] has been the decisive spiritual force in the history of Western civilization.... The papacy [is] the oldest continuing absolute monarchy in the world.... Roman Catholicism originated with the very beginnings of Christianity.... The Roman Catholic Church has maintained an unbroken continuity since the

---

[31] Mircea Eliade and C. J. Adams, eds., *The Encyclopedia of Religion*, vol. 12 (New York: Macmillan, 1987), pp. 430–431.

days of the Apostles, while all other denominations ... are deviations from it.... The two factors that are often regarded as the most decisive [for accounting for the emergence of Roman Catholicism] ... are the primacy of St. Peter ... and the identification of Peter with the church of Rome.[32]

From the *Handbook of Denominations*:

For the first 1,500 years of Christianity's history, the Western world was almost solidly Roman Catholic.... The Roman Catholic Church dates its beginning from the moment of Christ's selection of the apostle Peter as guardian of the keys of heaven and earth and chief of the apostles, and it claims the fisherman as its 1st Pope.... The faith and doctrine of Catholicism are founded upon that deposit of faith given to it by Christ and through his apostles, sustained by the Bible and by Tradition.[33]

From the *National Encyclopedia*:

The Church is the society founded by the God-Man Jesus Christ to carry on till the end of time his work for the salvation of mankind. On the eve of his departure from this world Christ delegated to his apostles his own threefold office of priest, prophet and king (Mt 28:18–20). After his Ascension, they and their successors were to teach, sanctify and guide mankind. He thus made the

---

[32] *Encyclopedia Britannica Online*, s.v. "Roman Catholicism," accessed March 30, 2024, https://www.britannica.com/topic/Roman-Catholicism.

[33] Frank S. Mead, *Handbook of Denominations in the United States*, ed. Samuel S. Hill (Nashville, TN: Abingdon Press, 1990), p. 215.

Church the ordinary medium of salvation for all men.... Since the Church has been commissioned by Christ to teach all revealed truth, every Catholic considers it his duty to accept her teaching(s).... Christ founded the Church when, a year before his death, he said to Simon, son of Jonas: "Thou art Peter, and upon this rock I will build my Church, and the gates of hell shall not prevail against it" (Mt 16:18). After his resurrection he confirmed Peter as the visible Supreme Head of this Church when he said to him: "Feed my lambs, feed my lambs, feed my sheep" (Jn 21:17).[34]

From *The Complete Guide to Christian Denominations: Understanding the History, Beliefs and Differences*:

Testament churches were governed by a plurality of elders (1 Timothy 5:17; 1 Peter 5:1). One of these elders typically rose to a position of authority over the others.... This individual came to be known as a bishop, this hierarchy facilitated the practical running of the church.... The bishop of the city exercised authority over all the congregational elders of the city.... Some bishops attained greater authority than others.... The bishop became prominent because the city in which the church was located was prominent. This was the case in Alexandria, Antioch, Rome and Carthage.... The bishop of Rome eventually became the head of the entire church. A number of factors led to this development. First, as the capital of the empire, Rome was strategically located ("all roads lead to Rome"). Further, this was the only Western church to have received

---

[34] *National Encyclopedia*, Pub. Leonard Melley, 1935, vol. 8 (Educational Enterprises), p. 514.

an epistle from the apostle Paul. Still further, Catholics believe Peter took up residence in Rome in AD 42, became its first bishop, and remained there until martyrdom in about AD 67. When Jerusalem fell and was decimated in AD 70, Rome's authority was further enhanced. Add to this the fact that the Roman church had attained significant wealth and great power, and one can easily perceive how Rome's bishop was destined for greatness.[35]

From **The Oxford Dictionary of the Christian Church**:

From an external point of view Roman Catholicism presents itself as an organized hierarchy of bishops and priests with the Pope as its head. This structure has been built up during a long history and rests its claims on the powers entrusted by Christ to His Apostles in general (Jn 20:23) and to St. Peter in particular (Mt. 16:18f; Lk 22:32; Jn 21:15–17), as whose successors the Popes are traditionally regarded.[36]

In **The Oxford Dictionary of Popes** (1986), Professor J. N. D. Kelley states in his introduction which appears on the inside front cover of the book:

The Papacy is the oldest of all Western institutions with an unbroken existence over almost 2,000 years. For much of its history, from early struggles to establish the primacy of

---

[35] Ron Rhodes, *The Complete Guide to Christian Denominations: Understanding the History, Beliefs, and Differences* (Eugene, OR: Harvest House, 2015), pp. 107–108.

[36] *The Oxford Dictionary of the Christian Church*, ed. F. L. Cross and E. A. Livingstone, 3rd rev. ed. (Oxford: Oxford University Press, 2005), s.v. "Roman Catholicism," p. 1418.

the See of Peter to the development of the modern papacy in the 20th century; spiritual and temporal powers have been inextricably mingled in the person of the Pope."[37]

The graph in chapter 3 of this book notes that Judaism is the seed of the true religion. The Roman Catholic Church stems directly from Judaism.

Ann Landers, a once-prominent national syndicated columnist, wrote an article that appeared in the Chicago Tribune on November 11, 1996. The title of the article was titled "Faith facts may surprise some people." She starts with the question: "Do you have any idea when your religion was founded and by whom?" She then lists the religions and their founders starting from Judaism (founded by God and His covenant with Abraham) approximately 4,000 years ago up through modern day America.

For instance, "If you are Lutheran," she says, "your religion was founded by Martin Luther in 1517." Or: "If you are Baptist, you owe the tenets of your religion to John Smyth, who launched it in Amsterdam in 1607." Finally, Landers concludes: **"If you are Roman Catholic, Jesus Christ began your religion in the year 33."**

In *World Religions Made Easy*, John Hunt and Mark Water state, "Through Peter, Jesus started a chain of authority that has extended in an unbroken line to the present Pope."[38]

In Spring of 1993, Ken Samples, a Protestant apologist, wrote an article in the ***Christian Research Institute Journal: What Ye Think of Rome?* (part 2)**:

---

[37] Oxford: Oxford University Press, 1986. Professor J. N. D. Kelley is a well-known Protestant historian, Anglican canon lawyer, fellow of the British Academy, and fellow of the Academic Council of Ecumenical Institute in Jerusalem.

[38] John Hunt and Mark Water, *World Religions Made Easy* (Chattanooga, TN: AMG, 2002), p. 36.

Catholicism, on the other hand, is the largest body within Christendom, having almost a two-thousand-year history (it has historical continuity with apostolic, first century Christianity), and is the ecclesiastical tree from which Protestantism originally splintered....

Those who classify Roman Catholicism as a cult (an inauthentic and invalid expression of Christianity) usually also give the Eastern Orthodox church the same classification. What they do not realize ... is that if both of these religious bodies are non-Christian, then there was no authentic Christian church during most of the medieval period. Contrary to what some Protestants think, there was no independent, nondenominational, Bible-believing church on the corner (or in caves) during most of the Middle Ages. Additionally, the schismatic groups who were around at the time were grossly heretical. So much for the gates of hell not prevailing against the church (Matt. 16:18).[39]

From *Illustrated World Encyclopedia* (1967):

The Roman Catholic Church is the largest of all Christian churches. The Church is governed by a hierarchy.... At the head of the hierarchy is the Pope, the leader of the Catholic Church on earth. Under him are the bishops. The Papacy (office of the Pope) and Episcopate (office of bishops) are considered to have been set up by Jesus, who appointed the Apostles as the first

---

[39] Kenneth R. Samples, *What Think Ye of Rome? Part Two: An Evangelical Appraisal of Contemporary Catholicism*, Christian Research Institute, chrome-extension://efaidnbmnnnibpcajpcglclefindmkaj/https://www.equip.org/PDF/DC170-2.pdf, pp. 3–4.

bishops and St. Peter as the 1st Pope or head of the Church.[40]

From *Reader's Digest, After Jesus: The Triumph of Christianity* (1992):

> Ignatius (of Antioch) had been the bishop of the church in Antioch for 40 years when he was denounced as a Christian during a short but intense period of persecution in the reign of Emperor Trajan.... Ignatius was cross-examined by the emperor himself and still refused to follow Trajan's orders to worship Roman deities. No doubt Trajan thought to make an example of this zealous Christian bishop, who was probably a converted pagan. Ignatius, who was about 70 years old, was given a brutal sentence: he was to be bound in chains and taken to Rome, where he would be devoured by beasts for the entertainment of the public. Unafraid, Ignatius regarded his punishment with joy ... when he reached Rome, Ignatius was devoured by two ferocious lions in the Flavian Amphitheater. (pp. 112–113)

Ignatius, knowing that he was to be martyred in Rome, quickly penned seven letters to the churches, very much like St. Paul did while he himself was in captivity as a prisoner. In these letters, Ignatius described the universal character of the Church.

In his Letter to the Ephesians, he quotes St. Paul: "**[You were] built upon the foundation of the apostles and prophets, Christ Jesus himself being the cornerstone, in whom the whole building is joined together and grows into a holy**

---

[40] *Illustrated World* Encyclopedia vol. 12, Bobley Publishing (1967), p. 4147.

temple in the Lord; in whom you also are built into it for a dwelling place of God in the Spirit" (Eph. 2:20–22; emphasis added).

He also states that bishops continue to be "**appointed the world over.**"[41] In Ignatius's letter to the Smyrnaeans, he employed a phrase new to Christian writings up to this point, marking this particular letter as one of the most significant documents of the early Church. He wrote, "**Wherever the bishop shall appear, let the multitude [of the people] also be; even as, wherever Jesus Christ is, there is the Catholic Church.**"[42] Here is a bishop who is going to his martyrdom death and ensuring that the messages about the Church remain intact for all to read and know.

Rather ironically, Martin Luther himself admitted that the Catholic Church is the true Church of Christ in a sermon:

> Accordingly, we concede to the **papacy** that they **sit in the true Church,** possessing the office instituted by Christ and inherited from the apostles, to teach, baptize, administer the sacrament, absolve, ordain etc. just as the Jews sat in their synagogues or assemblies and were the regularly established priesthood and authority of the Church. **We admit all this** and do not attack the office, although they are not willing to admit as much for us; yea, we confess that we have received these

---

[41] William Jurgens, *Faith of the Early Fathers*, Liturgical Press vol. 1 (Collegeville, 1970), p. 1; emphasis added.

[42] St. Ignatius of Antioch, Letter to the Smyrnaeans, in *Ante-Nicene Fathers*, vol. 1, ed. Alexander Roberts, James Donaldson, and A. Cleveland Coxe, trans. Alexander Roberts and James Donaldson (Buffalo, NY: Christian Literature, 1885, rev. online ed. Kevin Knight: New Advent), https://www.newadvent.org/fathers/0109.htm, chap. 8; emphasis added.

things from them, even as Christ by birth descended from the Jews and the apostles obtained the Scriptures from them."[43]

Martin Luther also remarked: "We concede — as we must — that so much of what they [**the Catholic Church**] say is true; that the **papacy has God's word and the office of the apostles, and that we have received Holy Scriptures, Baptism, the Sacraments, and the pulpit from them. What would we know of these things if it were not for them?**"[44]

In *Why I Became a Catholic,* published by Roman Catholic Books (1953), **Eugenio Zolli**, the former Jewish rabbi of Rome brilliantly states common sense as he shares:

> "But why didn't you join one of the Protestant Denominations, which are also Christian?" Zolli responds, "Because protesting is not attesting. I do not intend to embarrass anyone by asking: Why wait 1,500 years to protest? The Catholic Church was recognized by the whole Christian world as the true Church of God for 15 consecutive centuries. No man can halt at the end of those 1,500 years and say that the Catholic Church is not the Church of Christ without embarrassing himself seriously. I can only accept the Church which was preached to all creatures by my own forefathers, the Twelve [apostles] who, like me, issued from a Synagogue...."

---

[43] *Second Sermon for the Sunday after Christ's Ascension, John 15:26–16:4, A Sermon by Martin Luther,* in *The Sermons of Martin Luther,* vol.III (Yaren from his Church Postil, 1522), pp. 254–271; all emphases added.

[44] Martin Luther, *Sermon on the Gospel of St. John (1537),* chaps. 14–16 in *Luther's Works,* vol. 24 (St. Louis, MO: Concordia, 1961), p. 304; all emphases added.

We discussed the leaders of the Protestant reformers along with their man made theories and motivations. The Protestant reformers refer to two pillars called "sola scriptura" and "sola fide" as the formal and material principles of the reformation, respectively employing a classic Aristotelian and medieval distinction between the two. What they meant was "sola fide" was the "stuff" or "matter" of the Christian message, while "sola scriptura" its parameters or "form." Catholicism rejects both principles as well intentioned but misguided misunderstandings of what Scripture teaches on these two topics. Dr. Gerry Matatics, a former Presbyterian minister who converted to Catholicism stated: "In my own experience, when, upon a deeper study of Scripture, Sampson like, I leaned against these two principal pillars (of Protestantism) and the palace of Protestantism came crashing down."

So then, why are there so many Protestant denominations and thus tens of thousands of Christian denominations? Once one accepts *sola fide* or *sola scriptura* the answer is simple: private interpretation and private revelation. This is the main cause of all disunity among the various Christian denominations. The hallmark of Protestantism is to interpret Scripture individually. But the Bible can be rightly interpreted, and it can be wrongly interpreted. St. Paul writes, "Remind them of this, and charge them before the Lord to avoid **disputing about words, which does no good, but only ruins the hearers. Do your best to present yourself to God as one approved, a workman who has no need to be ashamed, rightly handling the word of truth.**" (2 Tim. 2:14–15; all emphases added). Indeed, even Satan can quote Scripture out of context (see Matt. 4:1–11). Within the Catholic Church, there is no deviation on the apostolic meaning of the Scriptures.

Remember that Catholics base their faith on Sacred Scripture (seventy-three books), Sacred Tradition (see John 20:29–31; 21:25; 2 Thess. 2:15–17), and Magisterium empiricism. Within the term *Sacred Tradition* is included the concept and meaning of the word *Trinity*. In fact, the Bible itself is a written form of its Sacred Tradition. When all three work together comprehensively, matters of authoritative teachings regarding the Deposit of Faith are immutable despite historic cultural or political affronts by men, nations, or political movements. Nonetheless, America continues to see churches pop up based upon Scripture alone (sixty-six altered books) and personal interpretations of its meaning.

We will close this chapter again with the words of St. Augustine, bishop of Hippo. Also during his time, heretical sects were forming and attempting to splinter away from the Roman Catholic Church. This is from his classic writing *Of True Religion*, in which he vehemently defends that there was, is, and ever shall be only one Church and Christian religion. He wrote this concerning God's only Church:

> We must hold fast to the Christian religion and the **communion of the Church which is Catholic** and is called Catholic not only by its own members but also by its enemies. Whether they will or not, heretics and schismatics use no other name for it than the name of Catholic, when they speak of it not among themselves but with outsiders. They cannot make them understood unless they designate it by this name which is its universal use."[45]

---

[45] Willam A. Jurgens, *The Faith of the Fathers* (Collegeville: Liturgical Press, 1970), p. 40; emphasis added.

REFLECTIONS

1. Who named your church and why?

2. Can churches that have differing doctrines on justification, salvation, sanctification, and ecclesiology comprise the one Body of Christ?

3. From whom did your church receive its teaching authority?

4. How many different "churches" have you explored?

Chapter 6

The Church as the Living Bride of Christ

*Jesus said to her, "Woman, believe me, the hour is coming when neither on this mountain **nor in Jerusalem** will you worship the Father. **You worship what you do not know; we worship what we know, for salvation is from the Jews**." (John 4:21–22; all emphases added)*

Jesus Christ, as God Himself, tells two very important facts to the woman at the well. First, correct worship of God the Father will soon no longer occur in Jerusalem; and the mountain reference refers to the mountain upon which pagan temples were constructed at the time Jesus walked the earth. Secondly, and most importantly, Jesus states that "we" worship what we *know*, meaning the God of Israel is the true and only living God. Jesus concludes with absolute clarity, "For salvation is from the Jews."

So, if salvation is from the Jews as Jesus said, how does this get conveyed to the modern Church? The word used in the original Greek Old Testament for "Israel in the wilderness" is the word *ekklesia*, the same word that the New Testament Gospels use for the word *church*. Therefore, the same word is used in both the Old Testament and that New Testament.

Prophecy of Mary

It is worth noting that the Old Testament is full of writings describing Israel as a "wandering daughter" whom God is calling back to Himself. In fact, these words are a prophecy of God's chosen Bride who is to start His Christian Church and cause a New Covenant to be made by God with humanity. It is the prophecy of Mary, the Jewish Mother of Jesus Christ, Spouse of the Holy Spirit, and Daughter of the God of Israel. She had to be Jewish.

"How long wilt thou be dissolute in deliciousness, O wandering daughter? For the Lord **hath created a new thing upon the earth: WOMAN SHALL COMPASS A MAN**" (Jer. 31:22, DRA; all emphases added). If you research the Douay-Rheims version, the text "A WOMAN SHALL COMPASS A MAN" is in fact comprised of all capitalized letters! Some may think that God's creation story was a one-and-done thing and only addressed in Genesis. Well, God is constantly creating—look to the Heavens for proof. Here God says that He will create something **new on earth post-Genesis—woman shall compass a man.** Mankind fell through a woman (Eve). Mankind will be restored through a woman (Mary). The Son of God chose His Mother before the beginning of time.

St. Jerome wrote that this sentence is the image and reference to the Infant Jesus enclosed in Mary's womb. Throughout his writing, the prophet Jeremiah uses beautiful marital imagery in his descriptions of a restored Israel. Did you ever wonder why Jesus refers to His mother as "Woman"? It is because that was Eve's name **before** the fall. *Woman* in the Greek Septuagint can translate to "wife" or an unmarried woman. Nonetheless, it is a term of endearment and respect for a female. Therefore although her human name was Mary, Jesus always refers to her as "Woman." Remember, Jesus has two natures: human and divine, but of one essence simultaneously. Well, if

God created Adam originally from the dirt and woman from Adam, then in Genesis, God originally created only man and from that man, woman came to be.

So, what does Jeremiah's recorded prophecy mean? If man fell through the initial causality of the disobedience of a woman in the garden, then God must restore mankind to Himself through a woman, one who would give birth to the sinless, perfect Man who would also have to go through immolation for all mankind's sins in order to restore us with God, the Father. The word *compass* is a transitive verb, meaning "to devise or contrive often with craft or skill" or "to bring about, achieve, or accomplish something; to obtain." This definition is from merriam-webster.com meanings (1) and (3, a, b). God said it, we didn't. He will create a man from a woman, and from this Man who is the Christ, Israel will be restored (see Matt. 15:24), so that in and through the Church, now called the Israel of God, the entire world may have salvation in His Name (the Gentiles included).

Jeremiah 31 should be read in its entirety. It is the *only* place in the Old Testament that the words *New Covenant* appear. After God says that He will create something new on earth — namely, bringing about and accomplishing with craft and skill the perfect, sinless man of divine origin created and housed within a *woman* — He states that only then will He declare a *New Covenant*: "Behold, the days are coming, says the Lord, when I will make a new covenant with the house of Israel and the house of Judah.... But this is the [new] covenant which I will make with the house of Israel after those days, says the Lord" (Jer. 31:31, 33).

To add further support to these Scripture verses, we turn to the New Testament. Biblical scholars ponder who first documented the Incarnation of the Word made flesh (Jesus Himself) in the New Testament. Many will answer St. Luke. The correct answer is St. Paul, who we know trained Luke to a great degree. We also know that

Paul's knowledge of the gospel is not of man but of divine origin, as he states in Galatians 1:11–12. His knowledge was given to him by divine revelation from the glorified Jesus Himself. Notice what St. Paul shares in Galatians: the first written words describing what God did to whom and why concerning the Incarnation of the Word made flesh. It matches the prophecy that Jeremiah wrote about Mary, Jesus, and salvation for the entire human race.

"But when the fulness of the time was come, God sent his Son, **made of a woman**, made under the law: That he might redeem them who were under the law: that we might receive the adoption of sons" (Gal. 4:4–5, DRA; emphasis added). St. Paul says a lot here. Let us unpack it: 1) in God's perfect timing, God would send His Son; 2) He was to be a man made of a *woman* who was under the Jewish Law — Mary; and 3) their Son would redeem Israel and the Gentiles would receive their adoption as sons (and daughters) of God — the Abrahamic Covenant. Direct and straightforward, yet it needed unpacking. So, why would God even need a woman? Because Jesus had to have a human nature. His human nature was given to Him by His Mother, the "Woman," Mary. She gave Him His blood, His human tissue, and His physical heart. These human bodily components are critically necessary for the immolation of Our Lord, the atoning sacrifice for you and me. Without Mary, there would be no blood to be shed for sin, no heart to pierce, and no flesh to scourge and crucify. Mary provided Jesus' human nature and God provided His Son's divine nature, and the Paschal Lamb came to be for our salvation. From Eve all mankind fell and from Mary's womb mankind is restored to eternal life in Jesus who is son of Mary (Mark 6:3) and Son of God.

How does the word *church* tie into these prophecies and the New Covenant? Forty-seven times the word *ekklesia* is found in the Old Testament, and every time it means but *one* way of worshiping the Lord before the coming of Christ. That was the Jewish Church, the religion, and the Law of Moses established by God. In the New Testament, Matthew mentions the Church (*ekklesia*) twice from Our Lord's own speech. In the book of Acts, the word *church* is mentioned twenty-four times, and in all the other epistles the word *church* is used sixty-eight times. Everywhere its meaning is the *one* Church of God in Christ pastored by the apostles who were hand-chosen by Christ. This is the true assembly or congregation of Christians who worship Him in the religion that is the natural extension of Judaism: the faith of the Nation of Israel, the Old Testament Chosen People. This echoes Jesus' previous words: "We worship what we know, for salvation is from the Jews" (John 4:22).

"Israel according to the flesh, which wandered as an exile in the desert, was already called the Church of God. So likewise the new Israel which while living in this present age goes in search of a future and abiding city is called the Church of Christ."[46] "Thus the Apostles were the first budding-forth of the New Israel, and at the same time the beginning of the sacred hierarchy."[47] Furthermore, the *Catechism of the Catholic Church* states:

> The word "Church" means "convocation." It designates the assembly of those whom God's word "convokes," i.e., gathers together to form the People of God, and who themselves, nourished with the Body of Christ [the consecrated Eucharist], became the Body of Christ.
>
> The Church is both the means and the goal of God's plan: prefigured in creation, prepared for in the Old Covenant, founded by the words and actions of Jesus Christ,

---

[46] Vatican Council II, Dogmatic Constitution on the Church *Lumen gentium* (November 21, 1964), no. 9.

[47] Vatican Council II, Decree on the Mission Activity of the Church *Ad gentes* (December 7, 1965), no. 5.

fulfilled by his redeeming cross and his Resurrection, the Church has been manifested as the mystery of salvation by the outpouring of the Holy Spirit. She will be perfected in the glory of heaven as the assembly of all the redeemed of the earth (cf. Rev 14:4).

The Church is both **visible and spiritual**, a hierarchal society and the Mystical Body of Christ. She is one, yet formed of two components, human and divine. That is her mystery, which only faith can accept.

The Church in this world is the sacrament of salvation, the sign and the instrument of the communion of God and men. (CCC 777–780; emphasis added)

This is why Christ's Church that He established is His Bride. God is preparing His Bride to one day meet her Bridegroom in eternity. We would encourage the reader to read the *Catechism of the Catholic Church* 751 to 780 to understand how Christ's Church currently exists on her pilgrimage in the world. The Catholic Church is both visible and spiritual. The spiritual aspect is a result of being guided by the Holy Spirit over human time until Jesus comes again. The apostolic Church is what St. John sees as a new Heaven and a new earth unfolding as Christ conquers and reigns forever. St. John states, "And I saw the holy city, **new Jerusalem**, coming down out of heaven from God, **prepared as a bride adorned for her husband**" (Rev. 21:2; all emphases added).

Remember that God makes covenants with men, covenants which are sacred family bonds (oaths). The gates of Hell will not prevail against His Church, the Roman Catholic Church, which has been guided almost two thousand years by the Holy Spirit. He knew also exactly when His Church would be established and who He would choose to be stewards of His divine will for His Bride. Just like the wedding vow between a bride and her bridegroom: "What therefore God has joined together, let not man put asunder" (Mark 10:9). God created a Church for all humanity to be joined to Himself in spiritual communion; Jesus is the Bridegroom and the Catholic Church is His Bride.

The Holy Land

In the Holy Land, wherever Jesus walked or did something significant mentioned in the Holy Bible, there is a Catholic Church or an Orthodox Church (which used to be a Catholic Church before A.D. 1054). Millions of people, including many non-Catholic Christians, travel there to walk in the footsteps of Jesus, Our Lord. Why is the Holy Land peppered with Catholic Churches? Because it is the original Church founded by Jesus Christ. We will go over a few small examples:

Where was Mary, the Mother of Jesus and the Daughter of St. Joachim and St. Anne, born?

The Blessed Virgin Mary was born in Jerusalem, in a cave near the Bethesda Pool. This became the home of St. Joachim, St. Anne, and Holy Mary for a short time before they moved to the city of Nazareth in the region of Galilee. This cave has been incorporated into the Church of St. Anne, named after Jesus' Grandmother.

Where did the angel Gabriel announce to Mary that she would be the Mother of God?

The exact location houses the Basilica of the Annunciation in Nazareth. It is one of the largest and most magnificent Churches in the Holy Land. Nazareth is known as the home of Mary, the Virgin Mother of Jesus.

This is the city where Jesus lived for thirty years with His parents and learned His trade as a carpenter and a mason.

Where did Mary physically visit her cousin Elizabeth, where John the Baptist leapt in her womb upon Mary's greeting?

In the idyllic village of Ein Karem, which is on the west side of Jerusalem, the Church of the Visitation stands. The location marks the spot where John the Baptist's parents had a summer home. This is documented in Luke 1:39–56. It was here that Mary sang her canticle or Magnificat. It is also here where the infant John hid with Elizabeth when Herod ordered the execution of all male children under the age of two. Here also is where the Church of St. John the Baptist stands, marking the place of his birth.

Where did Mary and Joseph travel to when she was pregnant with Jesus?

Mary and Joseph traveled to Bethlehem for the census to register according to a decree from Emperor Augustus. While they were there, Mary gave birth to Jesus in Bethlehem (which means "House of Bread"). On that location of the birth of our Savior Jesus is the Church of the Nativity in Bethlehem. A star underneath the altar marks the spot of Jesus' birth.

Where did the angels announce to the shepherds that the Messiah was born?

This is the Church of the Shepherds' Field. It is east of Bethlehem. This is the location where the angels announced the birth of Christ to the shepherds. At this site, the angels began praising God by saying, "Glory to God in the highest, and on earth peace to men of good will" (Luke 2:14, DRA).

Where did the Holy Family go after Jesus was born in Bethlehem?

The Holy Family fled to Egypt. The location where they stayed is in modern-day Cairo. There stands the St. Sergius and St. Bacchus Coptic Orthodox Church. The Holy Family also stayed at another location in Cairo which now houses the Church of the Holy Virgin.

Where did the Holy Family go after Joseph was told to go back to the land of Israel by an angel of the Lord?

The Holy Family returned to Nazareth where they lived in a cave. Today, the Church of St. Joseph stands there.

Where was Jesus transfigured before Sts. Peter, James, and John simultaneously, with Moses and Elijah appearing?

The Transfiguration of Jesus is described in detail in Matthew 17:1–8, Mark 9:2–8, and Luke 9:28–36. St. Peter recounts this event as well in 2 Peter 1:16–18. The human Jesus transfigures radiant and glorified upon Mount Tabor in the lower region of Galilee. Today, a Catholic Church sits upon this location, the Church of the Transfiguration.

Where did Jesus stay when He went to Jerusalem?

When Jesus went to Jerusalem for the Passover celebration feast, according to the Bible, He stayed with some of his best friends, Mary, Martha, and Lazarus, in the town of Bethany. Yes, there is a Catholic Church there in Bethany today, called the Church of St. Lazarus.

How many Catholic Churches are there in Jerusalem today?

There are at least thirty-five Catholic or Orthodox Churches and monasteries in Jerusalem which serve about one million people. The crown jewel of all the Churches in Jerusalem is the Church of the Holy Sepulcher. *Sepulcher* means "a monument cut in rock or built of stone in which a dead person is laid and buried."[48] It is here that all historic events took place along with artifacts to prove the existence, death, and Resurrection of Our Lord Jesus Christ. Inside this Church is Calvary or Golgotha, the exact spot on the planet where Jesus gave up His Body and Spirit to God the Father for the atonement of our sins. Jesus' empty tomb where He was buried and resurrected is inside as well. So is Jesus' anointing stone, where Joseph of Arimathea, assisted by Nicodemus, wrapped Jesus' body and placed it in the tomb (John 19:38–42). The tombs of both Joseph of Arimathea and Nicodemus are also inside the church, just adjacent to the Jacobite Chapel. It was originally built by St. Helena, the mother of Emperor Constantine, in about A.D. 330.

---

[48] *Catholic Bible Dictionary*, Scott Hahn ed. (New York: Image, 2009), pp. 129–130.

(Doubters have questioned whether Christ was truly crucified and buried at this site, but no rival site is supported by *any* real evidence. Furthermore, archeology confirms that the other first-century tombs which are located and preserved inside the church have burial shafts dated from the time of Christ's death and Resurrection.)

Where did the Last Supper occur and where did the Holy Spirit descend upon the apostles at Pentecost?

Both events occurred in the same place. The night of His betrayal by Judas, Jesus shared His Last Supper with the apostles. He would be arrested later after His agony in the Garden of Gethsemane. The resurrected Christ told the apostles to stay in Jerusalem until He returned to convey the Spirit upon them so they could preach the gospel to the entire world. On Pentecost, the Holy Spirit descended like tongues of fire upon the disciples (Acts 2:2–3). This holy site is called the *Upper Room*, or the Cenacle. It is a small two-story structure on Mount Zion. As this is the site of the Last Supper, it is also the location where the priesthood was established.

When Jesus was about thirty years old He left His home in Nazareth and sought out John the Baptist. Why?

Jesus was baptized by John the Baptist to fulfill all righteousness, for He had a human nature like us. Jesus traveled south to the Jordan River. Jesus was baptized about nine kilometers north of the Dead Sea and east of Jericho. Today, on that spot, stands the Church of St. John the Baptist.

Where did Jesus begin His public ministry?

Jesus began His public ministry in Galilee. He lived in Capernaum with Peter for three years after He left his parents' home in Nazareth. Capernaum became His new hometown. Today, directly over Peter's home, there is a Catholic Church called the House of St. Peter.

Where did Jesus perform His first miracle?

Jesus performed His first miracle in the city of Cana at a wedding celebration. On that location, we have the Church of Cana of Galilee.

Walking in the footsteps of Jesus in the Holy Land will take you from one Catholic Church to another.

The Spiritual Aspect of the Church

The churches in the Holy Land are visible signs of Christ's impact and footprints on earth. The Roman Catholic Church is both visible and invisible. The invisible part is the spiritual body that transcends all human time and space. It is the spiritual component that is constantly guided by the Holy Spirit, the third Person of the Most Holy Trinity. The Church established by Our Lord and Savior Himself is the New Israel. He created a Church to worship Him as He commanded until He comes again. That is why the resurrected Christ promised the apostles that He would be with them until the end of the age (the end of human time). Since the apostles are mortal creatures and would die shortly thereafter, Jesus was guaranteeing His presence among and within them until He comes again. This is proof of apostolic succession and the invisible presence of God within the Catholic Church until He returns. When Jesus Himself returns as determined by God the Father, the current Heaven and earth will be destroyed by fire.

Virtually all Christians agree on this point. However, when Jesus has St. John describe the New Jerusalem (the City of Peace) coming down from Heaven for all eternity as the final destination for those whom God determines are worthy to be in His presence, we don't have nor can we obtain the right to claim this final victory on our false soteriology, our efforts or merits. This New Jerusalem is Jesus' Church built over human time. The foundation of this New Jerusalem is the twelve apostles that Christ Himself chose.

Let us review exactly what Jesus had St. John write describing the New City of Jerusalem. Note that it currently does not exist! It descends from Heaven itself at the end of human time. John is describing the true Church, Christ's Bride herself. As the Bridegroom, Jesus meets His Bride. This is the spiritual dimension of the Catholic Church that many do not understand because they have been told that their (building) church is the real church. Here is what St. John states will happen at the end of time marked by Christ's glorious return:

> Then I saw a **new heaven and a new earth; for the first heaven and the first earth had passed away, and the sea was no more**. And I saw the holy city, **new Jerusalem coming down out of heaven from God,** *prepared as a bride adorned for her husband*; and I heard a great voice from the throne saying, "Behold the dwelling of God [**the new Jerusalem**] is with men. He will dwell with them, and they shall be his people, **and God himself will be with them;** he will wipe away every tear from their eyes, and death shall be no more, neither shall there be mourning nor crying nor pain any more, for the former things have passed away."... Then came one of the seven angels

who had the seven bowls full of the seven last plagues, and spoke to me, saying, **"Come, I will show you the *Bride*, the *wife of the Lamb*"** [note that the Bride, God's Church, is specifically called Jesus' wife]. And in the Spirit he carried me away to a great, high mountain, and **showed me the holy city Jerusalem coming down out of heaven from God, having the glory of God.** ... It [the new Jerusalem] had a great, high wall, with twelve gates, and at the gates twelve angels, and on the gates the names of the **twelve tribes of the sons of Israel were inscribed**; on the east three gates, on the north three gates, on the south three gates, and on the west three gates. And the wall of the city had **twelve foundations, and on them the twelve names of the twelve apostles of the Lamb [Jesus]**." (Rev. 21:1–4, 9–14; all emphases added)

Remember that Our Lord told us to not be of this world and stated that He has overcome the world. Jesus preexisted time and space and knew how and when His *ekklesia* would exist long before men decided that they knew better than God how the Church was to be established. Jesus Himself chose both sets of twelve Jewish men: the twelve original tribes of Israel, represented by the twelve sons of Jacob, and the twelve (Jewish) apostles. This was and will always be the divine governance structure of our Almighty God who created each of us.

The foundation of the New Jerusalem is built upon the apostles chosen by Jesus Himself. This is why the spiritual nature of the Catholic Church is called the New Israel. Jesus, or *the Lamb* as St. John refers to Him, picked twelve Jewish men to work alongside Himself for the sake of the lost sheep of Israel, or Israel in the wilderness. In fact, He said this when a Canaanite woman came to Him asking for healing for her demon-possessed daughter. Jesus said, "I was sent only to the lost sheep of the house of Israel" (Matt. 15:24). God Himself also calls His people Israel "lost sheep" in Jeremiah 50:6.

Jesus did heal the Gentile woman's daughter because of her faith. Through faith in Christ, the Gentiles are coheirs to the Abrahamic Covenant. The Old Covenant Israelites failed to bear witness to the promise to Abraham, yet Jesus succeeded in rescuing Israel and all nations are now redeemed and salvation is available to all. St. Paul drives this point home specifically in Galatians 3:28–29, where he says, "There is neither Jew nor Greek, there is neither slave nor free, there is neither male or female; for you are all one in Christ Jesus. And if you are Christ's, then you are Abraham's offspring, heirs according to the promise."

The New Covenant that God promised to the house of Israel in Jeremiah 31:31 was fulfilled by God when He created a new creation upon the earth: woman compassing man and the birth of the Christ, God's Only Begotten Son born of the Virgin Mary (see Jer. 31:22, DRA). Our Lady is the most exalted and most holy member of the Bride of Christ. Jesus is the Bridegroom, and the Church which includes Mary is His Bride. His Bride, the Catholic Church, has continuously existed since He Himself established her upon the earth.

Further proof is in the visible Catholic Church herself that is the organization headquartered in Rome. The Roman Catholic Church is the oldest continuous organization ever on earth. She is literally built upon the tomb of St. Peter. Over the centuries she has witnessed the rise and fall of empires, philosophies, and scientific theories and yet remains intact on the same spot on the earth proclaiming the same gospel.

For two millennia, men and women have lived the drama of faith in Jesus. The life of the Church is more intriguing than any soap opera or fictional novel. She literally has martyred saints and egregious sinners. She has acted heroically — and cowardly. Yet despite all human failings, the Church is still the Bride of Christ. And she will still be standing at the end of time when Jesus comes again.

She will stand because she alone has been given the gifts of infallibility, indefectibility, and indestructibility. This is made evident when we look back at the most powerful men who have tried and failed to destroy Jesus' Bride, the Catholic Church, over the past two thousand years. Here is a partial list: Roman emperors; multiple heretics; Alaric, the Barbarian King; Attila the Hun; Genseric, the Vandal King; the Visigoth invaders; Mohammed, and the Muslim crusaders that fought for centuries; the corrupt kings of England; the Mongolians; Martin Luther, and all the Protestant reformers; Napoleon; King Mwanga; the Japanese imperialist shoguns (military dictators); the Chinese Ming Dynasty; Vladimir Lenin, and the Chinese Communist Party; Joseph Stalin; Adolf Hitler; Benito Mussolini; Primo de Rivera; Manuel Alana, and the Spanish Popular Front; Plutarco Calles; Pol Pot; Mao Tse Tung; Ho Chi Minh; Fidel Castro; Che Guevara; and many more. All have tried to destroy the Catholic Church but couldn't. These men lie smoldering in their graves as food for worms. The Catholic Church lives on.

Sinful Men and the Church

Of course, many bad people have been associated with the Catholic Church. Even some Church leaders have behaved scandalously, and sinful men have despoiled the Church. However, remember that God is a God of covenant. It is man who breaks covenant, not God. God's oath is *forever* — and He can use sinful men to accomplish His purposes (see *CCC* 600) Let us look to examples from the Holy Bible where the men whom God personally chose to fulfill His covenants on earth nevertheless were extremely sinful:

The Church as the Living Bride of Christ

1. Abraham was the rock out of which Israel is hewn (Isa. 51:1–2), the Father of the Covenant and the source of all blessing for all the nations (Gen. 12:1–3; 17:1–14; 22:15–19; Gal. 3:7–9, 26–29). Unfortunately, Abraham acted cowardly and shamelessly when he demanded that his wife Sarah bear false witness concerning her identity out of fear (Gen. 12:10–20; 20:1–18).

2. Noah, after his incredible faith in God and entering a covenant with God (Gen. 7–9), proceeded to get drunk and lay naked. His sons found him in this naked and drunken state. Shem and Japheth were so ashamed of their father that they walked backward into the tent and covered their naked drunken father, Noah. His sons walked in backward because they were ashamed and scandalized.

3. Jacob, whose name was later changed by God to Israel, was chosen by God, yet he obtained the blessing of Isaac, his father, through deception (Gen. 27:1–46).

4. Judah, through whom the kingship of Israel shall pass, married a pagan Canaanite and fathered three sons, two of whom God kills because of their sinful lives. After their deaths, Judah went to a prostitute, who was his daughter-in-law (Gen. 38:1–30; Lev. 20:13). Nevertheless, kingship descended on his descendants, and the Messiah, Jesus Christ, came from this lineage or tribe.

5. Aaron was the brother of Moses and the one chosen by God to be the High Priest. Only his sons had the right to high priesthood (Exod. 28–29; 32:25–29,

Lev. 8; Num. 3:10), yet Aaron was the one who made the golden calf, or idol, for the people of Israel to falsely worship (Exod. 32). Later, he and his sister Miriam rebelled and mutinied against their brother Moses (Num. 12).

6. The Levites rebelled against Moses and Aaron during the rebellion of Korah (Num. 16; 17:5; 18:1–7). Later in the history of Israel, the Levitical priests fell into sin many times, yet their authority was not taken away until the curtain of the Temple was torn from top to bottom upon the death of Jesus Christ. The authority of the corrupt Levitical priests can be found in Malachi 2:1–9. Even so, Our Lord Jesus affirmed the religious authority of the Sadducees, Pharisees, and the High Priest, Caiaphas, while asserting that they were all corrupt (Matt. 23:1–3; 27:51; John 11:47–53).

7. King David murdered to hide his adultery, yet the adulteress, Bathsheba, would become the mother of his son Solomon. Why was she not punished according to the Law of Moses (2 Sam. 11:1–12:25; Lev. 20:10)?

8. King Solomon had many wives in violation of God's law (Deut. 17:17; 1 Kings 11:1–13).

9. Jonah disobeyed God and went west rather than east. Only after being swallowed by a whale did he obey God and go to Nineveh. When he finally went to Nineveh, he cared more about his comfort than the souls of the people of Nineveh (see Jon. 4:9–11).

10. St. Peter ran away and denied Jesus three times, yet Jesus chose him to strengthen his brothers (Luke 22:31–33). Peter then declared that two liars were to die for their false witness. How many religious leaders are put to for death for telling a lie? Does this action of putting people to death disqualify Peter as the chief of the apostles (Acts 5:1–11)?

11. St. Paul lied to try and save his life in Acts 23:6–11. He was clearly on trial because he was and had been teaching people that observance of the Mosaic Law was no longer necessary and that the Gentiles could now be saved (see Acts 21:17–36; 22:20–22). He was not on trial for his belief in the resurrection, for he was a Pharisee himself and Pharisees believed in the resurrection of the dead. So, Paul lied and claimed that he was only on trial because he believed in the resurrection of the dead. Also, in Acts 16:3, Paul had Timothy circumcised in violation of the Council of Jerusalem (where he was present) and in violation of his own letters against Judaizers (see his Letters to the Romans and Galatians). This was an act of hypocrisy or at the very least of compromise. Did this disqualify St. Paul as an apostle?

12. The Holy Bible, the very Word of God, states that Paul is the greatest of sinners (1 Tim. 1:12–16; 1 Cor. 15:9; Eph. 3:8), yet he was personally chosen by Christ to be the greatest evangelist in the history of mankind. The man who really thought that he was doing God's will by destroying Christianity and Jesus' Church became the instrument that Jesus hand-selected to build His Church throughout the known world. St. Paul went from the persecutor of

> the Church and enemy of Christ to the apostle to the Gentiles. Even though St. Paul's gospel is the direct result of a personal revelation from Jesus Himself, he nonetheless checks in with the Church authorities to make sure that he has not run in vain (Gal. 1:1–12; Acts 15).

St. Paul could have gone off and started his own "church of Christ" based upon the divine revelations given to him by Jesus as well as the Church witnesses to back him up (Ananias, Peter, James, Timothy, Luke, Barnabas, etc.). But he didn't. The grace given to Paul included knowing and accepting the authority structure of the apostolic Church established by Christ while He walked the earth. Does any human being today dare to claim that his or her personal religious experience or conversion to Christ regardless of the Holy Spirit's intervention is greater than St. Paul's? He could have easily established small independent churches dedicated to Christ, but he didn't. In fact, he did the opposite. He preached, and through His authority demanded unity and consistency of liturgy and teachings amongst all churches and warned of false teachers constantly.

The Church established by Jesus is His Bride. Scripture is clear. There will be a new Jerusalem that comes down from Heaven itself. This is the Kingdom of Heaven. Jesus, the Bridegroom, will accompany His Bride, which is the Catholic Church that He established on earth. She is both spiritual (invisible and transcending human time — "until the end of the age") and visible. Remember, Jesus was resurrected when He said to Paul, "Why do you persecute *me*?"

As we earlier mentioned, Paul asked, "Who are you, Lord?" and He responded, **"I am Jesus, whom you are persecuting"** (Acts 9:3–5; emphasis added). Jesus had established His Church and St. Paul was persecuting His Living Body, His Living Church. St. Paul even approved the martyrdom of Stephen, one of the first deacons of Christ's Church. Based upon Christ's statement to Paul, one can logically conclude that to persecute Christ is in point of fact the same as persecuting His Church.

We will close with St. Paul speaking about human marriage and Christ's marriage to His Bride, the Catholic Church — the Church that Paul served as an apostle:

> Wives, be subject to your husbands, as to the Lord. For the husband is head of the wife as **Christ is head of the church, his body, and is himself its [the Church's] Savior. As the church is subject to Christ**, so let wives also be subject in everything to their husbands. Husbands love your wives, **as Christ loved the church and gave himself up for her [His Bride], having cleansed her by the washing of water with the word, that he might present the church to himself in splendor, without spot or wrinkle or any such thing, that she [His bride, the Church] might be holy and without blemish."** (Eph. 5:22–27; all emphases added)

REFLECTIONS

1. Can Jesus, the Bridegroom, have multiple brides?

2. Why are only Catholic or Orthodox Churches built on every sacred and holy site on earth that bears witness to the Messiah, Jesus Christ?

3. Why were the twelve apostles given authority to rule the twelve tribes of Israel, and why do they comprise the foundation walls of the Heavenly Kingdom?

4. Have you ever studied what the Catholic Church teaches as biblical Truth?

Chapter 7

Intelligent Dissent: The Cause of Disunity

> *They went out from **us**, but they were **not of us**; for if they had been of **us**, **they would have continued with us**; but they went out, that it might be plain **that they all are not of us**. But you have been anointed by the Holy One, and you all know. I write you, not because you do not know the truth, but because you know it, and know that no lie is of the truth. (1 John 2:19–21; all emphases added)*

IN ESSENCE, WHAT ST. John is saying is that the people who left His Church never really belonged with His Church (the Catholic Church); otherwise, they would have stayed with *us*. He concludes by telling members of the Church that they know the Truth.

We have thus far walked through human history and presented evidence of Jesus' one, holy, catholic, and apostolic Church. In chapter 6, we discussed how Jesus' Bride is the literal Catholic Church. Not many so-called "Christians" would disagree with this. One thing that we remind our Protestant brothers and sisters of is that Jesus is simultaneously human and divine. He has always been and always will be. Those of us who die in sanctifying grace will see Him as He is. And if His Church is His Bride, then to say that there are multiple brides would mean that Christ is polygamous!

Jesus Has Only One Bride

The Scriptures are crystal clear; Jesus has a singular Bride. He has only one Church, one Bride. Jesus is monogamous. Period. God's sixth Commandment is "Thou shall not commit adultery." Jesus simply repeats this in Luke and Matthew by saying, "Every one who divorces his wife and marries another commits adultery, and he who marries a woman divorced from her husband commits adultery" (Luke 16:1) and, "You have heard that it is said, 'You shall not commit adultery.' But I say to you that every one who looks at a woman lustfully has already committed adultery with her in his heart" (Matt. 5:27–28).

So, it would be against Jesus' human nature to have multiple brides or wives. It is also against His divine nature to have multiple brides. If you recall, as you read in chapter 6 of this book, St. John stated that he saw God sending down His Church (the New Jerusalem) "prepared as a bride adorned for her husband" (Rev. 21:2). Both Bride and Husband are singular. God does not change. Jesus Christ is the same yesterday, today, and forever.

It should be apparent to anyone that the exponential growth of singular churches in America is alarming and should be disturbing. As we have discussed, it is caused by our government's insistence on disunity of doctrines, assemblies, and religions which in turn results in unlimited numbers of state sponsored "churches." And the term *church* remains undefined in the United States. Many often cite the Apostles' Creed during their services; however, many substitute the word *universal* for the word *catholic* and rationalize that their church is somehow part of or affiliated with the Catholic Church. This is an unreasonable presumption.

There is nothing inherently wrong with Christian people getting together in a U.S. government pseudo-defined "church" to worship Jesus Christ and read the Bible. For God loves prayer and praising.

Intelligent Dissent: The Cause of Disunity

Some of these U.S. "churches" are simply praise and worship halls where people come together to worship, give thanks to, and praise the triune God. Amen. But they are not *ekklesia* (Greek), or the Church of the One triune God — for there is only *one* Bride. Protestants are referred to within the Church as "ecclesial communities." For Catholics, having the Holy Eucharist in a tabernacle and believing that this is the Real Presence of Jesus Christ (Body, Blood, soul, and divinity), this is the very definition of what is a Church.

The Catholic Church has not failed nor can she ever fail in her mission as the New Israel or Bride of Christ. For had she failed, so too would the words of Jesus Christ promising that **He would be with His Bride**, the Church, until the end of time and that the gates of Hell would not prevail against her. Thus, either the Catholic Church is the true Church or Christianity fails.

Jesus Is Not a Liar

St. John was the last living apostle. All the other apostles were dead when he wrote his letter to Jesus' Church; therefore, let us remember the words of St. John: "**We are of God.** Whoever knows God listens to **us**, and he who is not of God does not listen to **us**. By this we know the spirit of truth and the spirit of error." (1 John 4:6; all emphases added).

So, who is the *us* that St. John is referring to? These are the bishops that he and the other apostles appointed as their successors in the Catholic Church. The Holy Spirit, who has been with Christ's Bride since Pentecost, is truly of God. As Christians we believe that all the promises of Jesus given to His apostles are true; therefore, there could never have been an apostasy in the early Church nor by her Church Fathers and popes. To say that there was an apostasy means that one is calling Jesus Christ a liar, and certainly no Christian wants to entertain this thought for even a second.

The next theory that some believe is that the Holy Spirit descended upon the apostles and stayed until they passed away. Following this, the Holy Spirit somehow took a nap for about 1,500 to 1,600 years of human time and suddenly woke up and said, "Oops! I must fix the Church that I established," which led to the Protestant Reformation. To suggest that there is or was an apostasy in the Church Jesus Himself established means: 1) Jesus is a liar and couldn't keep His promises; 2) the Holy Spirit fell asleep and/or changed His mind; or 3) God is not all-powerful and does not keep covenant because the gates of Hell must have prevailed against His Church. All three views are sacrileges.

Roman Catholics believe that the Holy Spirit has been with the Church uninterrupted and perpetually since A.D. 33. We also believe that the Holy Spirit will be with and in God's Church until the end of time. Christendom means Christ's Kingdom. That is His Church. Only the Catholic Church has been under the same governance and management structure for approximately two thousand years.

Man's Knowledge of God Is Extremely Finite

Why then has man attempted to redefine the salvific plan God outlined with the creation of His Church founded upon the apostles? The answer lies in our understanding of the concept of *intellectual dissent*. God created every human being; and He also gave each one of us an intellect and free will. But regardless of how intelligent anyone is, he or she still possesses very finite knowledge compared to God. Very finite! As history has shown us, many men have attempted to rethink or redefine what God has already ordained.

Ironically, every post–A.D. 1517 Christian religion is man-made. In fact, the Greek word for the study of salvation is *soteriology*. It deals with these philosophical questions: Who is saved? By whom are they saved? From what are they saved? By what means are they saved? When a human being takes his or her finite intellect and uses his or her free will to voluntarily dissent from the common beliefs of Christ's Catholic Church, disunity is created. It is exactly what Satan, the enemy, desires. He feeds on division and seeks only separation and destruction of the human being and his soul.

New Churches Have Always Failed

Every new soteriology during the first one thousand years after Christ's death that was developed by human intellect and challenged the teachings of the Catholic Church has disappeared forever. Yes, all these heretics that have splintered off the Catholic Church are gone: Marcionism, Docetism, Montanism, Manicheanism, Donatism, Pelagianism, Arianism, Nestorianism, Sabellianism, and so forth. The oldest Protestant church was started around 1517. Most Evangelical or Fundamentalist-type non-denominations aren't even one hundred years old. We would surmise that like the sects of old, these too will disappear. This is the destiny of the Protestant sects: to start, to develop somewhat, and then to die off.

How can we say this? Because only the Church that was established by Christ (see Matt. 16:18–19) will last until the end of time (Dan. 2:44; 7:14; 2 Sam. 7:12–16). The reason that the Catholic Church is indestructible is because the Holy Spirit is the Soul of the Church (see *CCC* 809) and Jesus sustains the Church continually (see John 15:1–5; Acts 17:28–29) because she is His Body (Col. 1:18) and Bride (Eph. 5:21–31). We urge the reader to read the aforementioned Scripture references.

Fundamentalism

A main reason for the explosion of non-defined "churches" specifically in the United States is the recent movement of non-denominational churches. This non-denominational movement is also known as Fundamentalist Christianity. It was started about 1910 to 1915, and was funded by two wealthy oil industry brothers named Lyman and Milton Stewart of Niagara, Ontario, Canada. They believed that the various Protestant sects were becoming too progressive or liberal in their thinking and teachings, so they wished to simply refocus on conservative views that were based upon a biblical worldview.

Once again, Fundamentalist sects continue to divide from mainline Protestant churches. Fundamentalism quickly spread throughout the United States. The most well-known Fundamentalist denomination is Calvary Chapel, founded by Chuck Smith in 1965 in Costa Mesa, California. Unfortunately, too many people base their Christianity on their feelings. They often make statements like "I like this church because it makes me feel good"; "I like the music because I like to sing"; "I like the fellowship"; or "I like listening to the charismatic preacher."

But Christianity must not be based on feelings. Feelings are not the measure of reality or Truth.

Revivalism

Another movement which started in the nineteenth century and has fueled thousands of independent so-called "churches" is called *Revivalism*. Since the twentieth century, it is now referred to as *Pentecostalism*. Revivalism and Pentecostalism have brought another "feelings-based" approach to Christianity in the United States. They have as their emphasis the human heart (feelings) in contrast to the head (intellect and reason). They promote the idea of intense religious feelings, which further sentimentalizes American Christianity.

Their preachers, with their increased focus on human emotions, preach a feel-good message that titillates individual emotion. They will always state that this is because the Bible says so. They often promote prosperity as the means to solving all of your problems. Trust in God and He will save you from anything, including material destitution. With their message of emotional revival, they have become extremely attractive to women seeking affirmation because women are generally more emotional than men. Most garden-variety fundamentalist Christians are sincere people and generally love the Lord; however, their pastors are sciolous. To be sciolistic is to have a superficial knowledge and a shallow understanding of a topic. In other words, they have the affections of scholarship but are lacking in substance on the topic. But when the topic is the salvation of your soul, you should pay attention to the actual theology of salvation as taught by Christ's Church since He ascended in A.D. 33.

A lot of what we are witnessing today is simply social reform inside a building that happens to be called a "church." We all know Americans love individual freedoms. When individualism is mixed with religion the result is the proliferation of non-denominational churches which entertain our emotions. We Americans do love our entertainment; in fact, it is our *modus operandi* in the land of plenty. Whatever makes us feel good — let's do that. This includes our Christian churches. But again, one should not attend a church based on how it makes you feel.

Dissenting from the Truth

We all agree that God gave us our existence along with two other things as a result of this existence: intelligence and free will. Intelligence is the quality of insight or reason. It is also an aptitude for grasping truth through the relationships between facts and meanings. Intelligence sits at a higher natural order to God than emotion. In other words, emotion is a lower faculty than intelligence. But when intelligence produces dissent from the truth, it is not sound. Who was the first to dissent? It was Satan himself. He summarily rejected God's authority and continues to dissent to God's perfect plan for humanity through his activities that cause dissension amongst human beings.

This is the spiritual realm that many people do not recognize. The dissentious nature of the enemy is everywhere. It causes sin in our human nature, wars in our collective natures, and ultimately, the destruction of our souls if we succumb to sin. St. Paul said it very well, "For we are not contending against flesh and blood, but against the principalities, against the powers, against the world rulers of this present darkness, against the **spiritual hosts of wickedness in the heavenly places**" (Eph. 6:12; emphasis added).

It is indeed a spiritual battle. A battle for one's soul. Satan and his minions know full well the end of the story: they lose and Christ wins. Until Jesus Himself returns, this spiritual battle rages not figuratively but literally. Jesus and His angelic beings against Satan and his demons who err to follow. We are the prize. We, while living on earth, choose Heaven or Hell based upon the choices that we make with our intellect and free will. The principalities and powers are certain choirs or hierarchies of angelic beings that God made with infused intellectual knowledge and free will. These realms have two kinds of angelic beings: those who have submitted to God and Jesus' lordship and those who have dissented, becoming demons or fallen angels. The enemy really does thrive and enjoy dissension, for in dissension, one focuses on self-interest and not on God who is all in all. We too must submit to God's authority or reject His authority.

Harkening back to the great Protestant Revolt against Christ's Church: Luther, although a priest himself, dissented from the Church by not recognizing her spiritual authority over every human being until Christ comes again. But think about it: Luther was an intelligent man, yet he rebelled against Christendom and refused Church authority.

Fast-forward to today in the United States of America and many people are mere by-products of this event of dissension. Most Christians either follow what they were taught by their parents or ancestors, or become Christian based on the recommendations of family or friends. Few study human history on their own and form conclusions as to which church is the true Church of Christ.

We encourage you to do so. One person who did was St. John Henry Newman, a nineteenth-century convert to Catholicism from the Church of England. He summarized well the necessity of learning human history. He stated, "And this one thing at least is certain ... the Christianity of history is not Protestantism. If ever there were a safe truth, it is this ... to be deep in history is to cease to be a Protestant."[49] What St. Newman is saying is that Protestants who study Church history, especially the Church Fathers, most likely will conclude this simple truth: Jesus Himself started the Catholic Church. Pope Benedict XVI stated: "We cannot have Jesus without the reality He created, the Church."

St. Newman is not suggesting that those who study his maxim must enter the Church. What he means is that Church history argues against Protestantism. Those Christians who have accepted the gift of faith handed down through the apostles to today are called Catholic Christians. Those Christians who have voluntarily elected to

---

[49] John Henry Newman, *An Essay on the Development of Christian Doctrine* (South Bend: Notre Dame, 2015), pp. 7–9.

remain outside the Catholic Church because they have not accepted her authority or teachings are called Protestants.

Some dissenters enjoy making caustic arguments against Christ's Church to justify their choices in religious beliefs. Some churches actually have an explicit anti-Catholic message inherently embedded in their doctrine, though others have an implicit message to avoid her. The Catholic Church is also the primary religion attacked by the media, secular universities, politicians, and the entire culture itself. Anti-Catholicism is alive and well.

Unity and Continuity

It is easy to attack the Catholic Church because she is *one*. She is a monolith that no human has destroyed, albeit many have attempted to do so. The Catholic Church is a "city set on a hill" as noted in Matthew 5:14. So, it is really the disunity of our separated brothers and sisters that makes it difficult to achieve true unity as Christ commanded of His Church. Perhaps one day, these wayward, well-intentioned Christians will return to His one true Church as Christ our Savior intended. One thing is certain, the idea of one divinely founded Church, possessing supernatural guidance, unity of doctrine, authority from Jesus Himself, and continuity of dogmatic discipline is wholly lost among Protestant denominations. Why? Because the term *unity* as applied to Protestantism and its descendants has no significance to them. Christ's Body, the Catholic Church, becomes the universal donor for Christian religious sects.

It is easy to attack continuity and unity of purpose as given to Jesus' Church. This is especially true when one views the Catholic Church as a purely material and visible edifice. She is this and much more. She is also the mystical, spiritual Body of Christ.

How can we say this with any authority? Well, let's walk through what Scripture says along the way of the development of the Catholic

Intelligent Dissent: The Cause of Disunity

Church while we look for unity and continuity. The Church Jesus Himself established was organized under the guidance of the Holy Spirit (John 14:16–18; 16:13; Acts 2:1–4) and established upon the chosen twelve apostles (Luke 22:30). Peter was the preeminent apostle, and he was left with the authority of Jesus (the King) by virtue of his name change and the transfer of the keys with rabbinical powers conferred to him (Matt. 16:17–19). All apostles were conferred with authority as teachers and judges (Matt. 18:17–18), but Peter was left as the chief shepherd by Jesus Himself (John 21:15–17). The Church was let loose on earth once the Spirit, as promised by Jesus at the Last Supper, was set upon them at the Pentecost. Thus, this Church that Jesus Himself established is the final court of arbitration vested with His authority (1 Tim. 3:15). The Church that Jesus created upon the apostles has always been part of God's eternal plan in Christ Jesus.

Even the heavenly beings know that there is only one Church. St. Paul states, "To me ... this grace was given ... to make all men see the plan of the mystery hidden for ages in God who created all things; **that through the church the manifold wisdom of God might *now* be made known to the principalities and powers in the heavenly places**" (Eph. 3:8–10; emphasis added).

Let's look at unity and continuity after Pentecost. Here is what happened as the Church spread her influence through preaching and teaching the gospel:

1. James the Greater went to Spain and then back to Jerusalem, where he was martyred by Herod Agrippa.

2. John went to Ephesus (the first church to honor Mary, our Blessed Mother, built in Ephesus, Turkey in the second century).

3. Andrew went to Russia.

4. Bartholomew, or Nathanael, went to Persia.

5. Simon the Zealot and Thaddeus (Jude) also went to Persia.

6. Thomas went to India.

7. James the Lesser preached in Jerusalem and served as the bishop of Jerusalem until he was stoned by the Jews and then thrown off the Temple parapet wall. The Jews finally struck him on the head with a club and his body was cut to pieces with a saw. All this occurred in A.D. 62, because the Jewish leaders were worried about the growing number of believers in Jesus as the Christ. Jerusalem and the Temple were destroyed by God, who utilized the Roman army to do so in A.D. 70.

8. Matthew went to Persia.

9. Mark went to Egypt.

10. Philip went to Phrygia.

11. Matthias went to Ethiopia.

12. Peter and Paul went to Rome. These two men gave their lives as well for the gospel in Rome and the Church immediately installed a successor to the Bishop of Rome, who had preeminence over all his brother bishops. This unbroken apostolic succession is found only in the one, holy, catholic, and apostolic Church which remains headquartered in Rome.

St. Paul testifies that Crescens, one of the seventy-two disciples sent out by Jesus in Luke 10, was sent to Gaul, modern-day France (2 Tim. 4:10); however, Linus, whom he also mentions, was his companion in Rome (2 Tim. 4:21). Linus would be the successor to Peter in the episcopate of the Church. Peter ordained Anacletus, or Cletus as he is sometimes known, as a priest. He would serve as the third continuous Bishop of Rome. Clement would serve as the next Bishop of Rome, as St. Paul testifies that he was his co-laborer in Christ (Phil. 4:3). The episcopal chair has not been vacant during this final age.

Another interesting and important fact is that tradition and history teach that the seventy-two whom Jesus appointed through the laying on of his hands became bishops of the Church. This further supports the apostolic succession and authority of the Church. The reader is encouraged to research what became of the seventy-two men Jesus hand-selected.

Tertullian was a prolific Church Father who wrote extensively on the theology of the Church. In his *Demurrer against the Heretics* (ca. A.D. 200), he writes concerning the necessity of apostolic succession:

> If there be any [heresies] bold enough to plant themselves in the midst of the apostolic age, so that they might seem to have been handed down by the apostles ... we say to them: let them show the origins of their churches, let them unroll the order of their bishops, running down in succession form ... one of the apostles or of the apostolic men who continued steadfast with the apostles. For this is the way in which the apostolic Churches transmit their lists: like the Church at Smyrnaeans, which records that Polycarp was placed there by John; like the Church of the

Romans where Clement was ordained by Peter. Let the heretics invent something like it.⁵⁰

The Catholic Church Imitates Jesus Christ

But what is the best evidence that the Catholic Church was truly founded by Jesus Christ? The Catholic Church imitates Christ Himself as the God-Man in that she is the most hated Christian Church in the world. She has one sole purpose; namely, that the Kingdom of God may come and the salvation of humanity will be accomplished in, through, and with Jesus Christ. So naturally, as the Body of Christ, she too must follow the trials and tribulations of her Founder and Head, Christ Himself. His physical body endured merciless persecution and scourging: so also His Mystical Body, the Catholic Church, must endure the same sufferings and persecutions (see *CCC 675*)

What follows is a comparison between Jesus Christ and His Mystical Body. He is the Head, and His Church is His Body. For St. Paul writes, "And he [God] has put all things under his feet and has made him [Jesus] the head over all things for the church, which is his body, the fulness of him who fills all in all" (Eph. 1:22–23). You cannot separate the head from the body; the head and the body are one and whatever happens to one happens to the other. The unbelieving world hated Jesus despite all the signs that He was, in fact, the Christ. The unbelieving world hates the Catholic Church as well. Note the similarities:

---

⁵⁰ Tertullian, The Demurrer Against the Heretics, Chapter XXXII.

Intelligent Dissent: The Cause of Disunity

Jesus Persecuted (He — The Bridegroom)	The Church Persecuted (She — His Bride)	Bible Source
They rebelled against His authority.	They rebelled against her authority.	Acts 9:1–5
They said, "Crucify Him."	Heretics have tried to destroy her.	2 Peter 2:10
He is called Beelzebub.	They call the Church satanic.	Matthew 10:25
He is called a false Messiah.	They call her a false Church.	Luke 22:70–71
He called Himself the Son of God.	She claims that she was founded by God.	Matthew 16:18
He called Himself the Truth.	She claims to be the Pillar of Truth.	1 Timothy 3:15
He called Himself a king.	She claims to be His Kingdom.	Matthew 16:19
He could not sin.	She has no spot or wrinkle.	Ephesians 5:27
He was not believed by many.	She is not believed by many.	Luke 22:67
He was denied by many.	She is denied by many.	Luke 22:57–60
He was derided and not understood.	She is derided and not understood.	2 Peter 2:12
Not understanding Him, they walked away.	Not understanding her, they walk away.	John 6:66
He had false accusers.	She has false accusers.	Mark 14:56–5
He was mocked.	She is mocked.	Luke 23:35–37
He was hated without a cause.	She is hated without a cause.	John 15:18–25
His accuser, Judas, dies.	Her accusers die but she lives.	Ephesians 3:216
His enemies would stumble and fall.	Her enemies stumble and fall.	John 18:6 / Revelations 19:11–21

Jesus Persecuted (He — The Bridegroom)	The Church Persecuted (She — His Bride)	Bible Source
We have no king but Caesar.	We have no need of His Kingdom. We need the Bible alone.	John 19:15
He was rejected by men.	She has been rejected by the world	Matthew 16:21
He bore His Cross.	She also bears a cross.	Matthew 16:24
He died on the Cross.	She has thousands of martyrs for Him.	Revelation 6:9
Two thousand years later He lives.	Two thousand years later she lives.	
He has power over demons.	She has power over demons.	Luke 10:19
Can anything good come from Nazareth?	Can anything good come from Rome?	John 1:46
He was scandalized.	She is scandalized by laws and institutions.	CCC 2286

No matter how hard the persecutors try to overcome His Body, which is His Bride, His Kingdom will last forever (see Dan. 7:14; Heb. 1:8). His Body and Bride, the Church, will last until the end of the world. He promised this by saying, "teaching them to observe **all** that I have commanded you; and lo, **I am with you always, to the close of the age**" (Matt. 28:20; all emphases added).

Jesus Christ Himself warned us about the future persecutions of His Body in the final Beatitude:

> Blessed are you when men revile you and persecute you and utter all kinds of evil against you falsely on my account. Rejoice and be glad, for your reward is great in heaven, for so men persecuted the prophets who were before you." (Matt. 5:11–12)

Intelligent Dissent: The Cause of Disunity

Whenever you see or hear someone persecuting the Catholic Church or speaking falsely against her, seriously, be happy — rejoice! Those people are helping Catholics get to their eternal reward in Heaven. It is a promise of Jesus Christ Himself.

We will end this chapter with prophetic messages by Ven. Archbishop Fulton J. Sheen and G. K. Chesterton:

> If I were not Catholic and were looking for the true Church in the world today, I would look for the one Church which did not get along well with the world; in other words, I would look for the Church that the world hates. My reason for doing this would be, that if Christ is in any one of the churches in the world today, He must still be hated as He was when he was on earth in the flesh. If you would find Christ today, then find the Church that does not get along with the world. Look for the Church which is hated by the world, as Christ was hated by the world. Look for the Church which is accused of being behind the times, as Our Lord was accused of being ignorant and never having learned. Look for the Church which men sneer at as socially inferior, as they sneered at Our Lord because He came from Nazareth. Look for the Church which is accused of having a devil, as Our Lord was accused of being possessed by Beelzebub, the Prince of Devils. Look for the Church which, in seasons of bigotry, men say must be destroyed in the name of God as men crucified Christ and thought they had done a service to God. Look for the Church which the world rejects because it claims it is infallible, as Pilate rejected Christ because He called himself the Truth. Look for the Church which is rejected by the world as Our Lord was rejected by men. Look for the Church which amid the confusion of conflicting opinions, its members love as they love

Christ, and respect its voice as the very voice of its Founder, and the suspicion will grow, that if the Church is unpopular with the spirit of the world, then it is unworldly, and if it is unworldly, it is other-worldly. Since it is other-worldly, it is infinitely loved and infinitely hated as was Christ Himself. But only that which is Divine can be infinitely hated and infinitely loved. Therefore, the Church is Divine."[51]

It is impossible to be just to the Catholic Church. The moment men cease to pull against it they feel a tug towards it. The moment they cease to shout it down they begin to listen to it with pleasure. The moment they try to be fair to it they begin to be fond of it. But when that affection has passed a certain point it begins to take on the tragic and menacing grandeur of a great love affair."[52]

---

[51] Quoted in Frs. Rumble and Carty, *Radio Replies*, vol. 1 (St. Paul, MN: TAN, 1979), p. ix.
[52] G. K. Chesterton, *The Catholic Church and Conversion*, pp. 59–124 in *G. K. Chesterton: Collected Works*, vol. 3 (San Francisco: Ignatius Press, 1990), p. 92.

REFLECTIONS

1. Why do you believe what you believe?

2. Have you ever studied what the Catholic Church truly teaches?

3. Does your interpretation of Scripture differ from Christ's Church's teachings? If so, why?

4. What spiritual authority resides in your church? Are there divine witnesses to its purported "authority"?

CHAPTER 8

Do You Need Evidentiary Supernatural Proof?

*If I [Jesus Christ] have told you [Nicodemus]
earthly things and you do not believe, how can you
believe if I tell you heavenly things? (John 3:12)*

WE ALL LIVE IN the natural world created by God. This realm can only give birth to things that are in the natural order; human beings give birth to other human beings. However, Jesus wants us to focus on the spiritual realm. For it is in the spiritual realm that supernatural life exists. He is *the* living example. God the Father and His Son Jesus have one and the same divine nature. The Son is "one being with the Father.... He came down from Heaven by the power of the Holy Spirit. He became incarnate of the Virgin Mary and became man" (Nicene Creed). Despite having a human nature, He lives forever as the firstborn of the resurrected from the dead. All our hope rests in this promise of restoration and eternal life in Him.

Yet we are mere mortals created in God's image. We are not capable of achieving eternal life on our own. It is a gift or grace that we receive through our faith and hope in Jesus alone. This is what Jesus was trying to tell Nicodemus in John 3. People live and cherish their earthly existence and do not fully embrace that they too were born to die like Christ Himself.

Jesus died for one reason: **you**! We must also die, and He alone determines whether we live forever with Him in the Kingdom of Heaven. Alternatively, He will have us suffer the purgation of our venial sins and the effects of mortal sin that has been forgiven in Purgatory — for nothing unclean will ever enter the Kingdom (Rev. 21:27) — and He alone determines when we shall eventually be allowed a place in Heaven. If we commit mortal sin and don't repent, we are deprived of sanctifying grace, which causes exclusion from Heaven and eternal death in Hell (CCC 1861). Those who chose to serve self over God while in the body chose separation from their source of life. We all choose what we are destined to receive by the lives we live while in the body. St. Paul said this very well, "For we must all appear before the judgment seat of Christ, so that each one may receive good or evil, according to what he has done in the body" (2 Cor. 5:10).

So, while we exist in this natural realm in the human body, we should live with only one goal: to prepare to live with God forever in the Father's House (see John 14:2). This is challenging for us mortals because, in this natural realm, we process **all** information through five natural senses consisting of sight, hearing, touch, taste, and smell. This is how we live in the body. It is our intellect or reason that processes these senses and draws conclusions about whether what we encounter is good or evil. This is where our free will resides in both our intellect, or mind, and our conscience which is a faculty of the soul. One's soul is the spiritual principle of the human being. While we live in the body, the body and the soul comprise one human person. This is why Scripture is replete with passages regarding focusing on Heaven, the spiritual aspects of our true eternal existence, for example:

> That which is born of the flesh is flesh and that which is born of the Spirit is spirit. (John 3:6)

> For the mind that is set on the flesh is hostile to God; it does not submit to God's law, indeed it cannot; and **those who are in the flesh cannot please God**. But you are not in the flesh, you are in the Spirit, if the Spirit of God really dwells in you. Any one who does not have the Spirit of Christ does not belong to him. (Rom. 8:7–9; emphasis added)

> [Jesus said to the woman at the well,] "**God is spirit, and those who worship him must worship in spirit and truth**." (John 4:24; emphasis added)

We want to reiterate that the Church Jesus Christ established is both a visible Church and an invisible Church. She is His body of which He is the Head. This is analogous to our own body (visible) and soul (invisible). The *Catechism of the Catholic Church* 770 says, "The Church is in history, but at the same time she transcends it. It is only 'with the eyes of faith' that one can see her in her **visible reality *and*** at the same time in her **spiritual reality** as bearer of divine life" (all emphases added).

Let us briefly review four supernatural, or spiritual realm phenomena as proof that our living Jesus Christ resides in the Church that He established. These supernatural events have continued to occur *only* in the Catholic Church and Orthodox Church. Our goal is to show demonstrative evidence to confirm which Church has Jesus' true real presence. For He commanded us to worship Him "**in [our] spirit and truth**" (John 4:23, 24) and again, these only occur within the true Church, Roman and Eastern Orthodox.

Supernatural Proof #1: Eucharistic Miracles (Jesus' Constant Reappearing as Human Flesh and Blood)

> I am the living bread which came down from heaven; if any one eats of this bread, he will live forever; and the bread which I shall give for the life of the world is my flesh.... Truly, truly, I say to you, unless you eat the flesh of the Son of man and drink his blood, you have no life in you; he who eats my flesh and drinks my blood has eternal life, and I will raise him up at the last day. (John 6:51, 53–54)

The Eucharist in the Catholic Church is her greatest treasure. Jesus *literally* becomes the Bread of Life and is *fully present*; meaning His Body, Blood, soul, and divinity is truly present in the Eucharist Host. This occurs when the priest consecrates the Host during the Holy Mass by reciting the words of Jesus Himself during the Last Supper just as He broke the bread and gave it to them proclaiming that it was His Body. Similarly, the cup of wine became His Blood.

This supernatural phenomenon is known as *transubstantiation*. Transubstantiation is the change of the substance of bread and wine into the substance of the Body and Blood of Christ, so that only the accidents of bread and wine remain after the consecration by the priest. We are to eat His Body and drink His Blood if we wish to partake in eternal life. He is our Source of Life, and we can partake in this eternal life-giving food when we receive the Most Holy Eucharist. Sadly, many Catholics take for granted this gift that resides in the Catholic Church. It was this sacrificial remembrance that the early Church Fathers liturgically performed. To understand the enormity of the Catholic Mass, one must understand that the heavenly liturgy and the earthly liturgy are one and the same.

As Catholics, we participate in the Holy Mass that is the New Covenant on earth offered by Christ's priests. The reality of this is evident by the Church Fathers and continues to this day. The Church Fathers reference the prophecy of the now-fulfilled sacrifice of the pure offering of Christ Himself from Malachi 1:11: "For from the rising of the sun to its setting my name is great among [all] the nations, and in every place incense is offered to my name, and a pure offering; for my name is great among the nations."

This is the prophecy of the Catholic Mass. Only in the Catholic Church is this pure offering of the spotless, sinless lamb performed in every nation in human history, every hour on the hour, all around the world. Hence, from the rising of the sun until its setting incense is offered and the eucharistic Bread from Heaven is given for the spiritual sustenance of and permanent conferral of sanctifying grace upon souls; therefore, the consecrated Bread and the Precious Blood are given utmost adoration, as this is Almighty God Himself. Jesus is truly present, and we worship Him alone in spirit and truth. It is the preeminent Sacrament in the Catholic Church, as it is Jesus Himself.

Many other Christian churches refer to this as "communion," "the Lord's Supper," or "the breaking of the bread." These other Christian churches commonly believe that this partaking is only symbolic, though others believe that they too can somehow make the common elements of bread and wine, or grape juice, Jesus Himself by thinking it so and by going through a non-Catholic Christian religious ritual. These human opinions that Christ is only in these elements as a "sign," symbolically, or somehow was received elsewhere without proper consecration by apostolic succession were rejected at the Council of Trent (session 13, can. 1, 6, 8).

The apostolic Church Fathers have all held consistent beliefs. Here are but a few quotes:

St. Ignatius of Antioch, Disciple of St. John the Apostle

Take heed, then, to have but *one* **Eucharist**. For there is one flesh of our Lord Jesus Christ, and one cup to [show forth] the **unity** of His blood; one altar, as there is one bishop, along with presbytery and deacons, my fellow-servants: that so, whatsoever you do, you may do it according to [the will of] God.[53]

You should regard the **Eucharist as valid which is celebrated either by a bishop** [in the apostolic Church], **or by someone he authorizes** [ordains as a priest].[54]

St. Justin Martyr

And this food is called among us the **Eucharist**, of which no one is allowed to partake but the man who believes that the things which we teach are true [Catholic doctrine], and who has been washed with the washing that is for the remission of sins, and unto regeneration, and who is so living as Christ has enjoined. For not as common bread and common drink do we receive these; but in like manner as Jesus Christ our Saviour, having been made flesh by the Word of God, had both flesh and blood for our salvation, so likewise have we been taught that the food which is blessed by the prayer of His word, and from which our blood and flesh by transmutation are nourished, is the

---

[53] St. Ignatius of Antioch, Letter to the Philadelphians, in *Ante-Nicene Fathers*, vol. 1, https://www.newadvent.org/fathers/0108.htm, chap. 4; all emphases added.

[54] St. Ignatius of Antioch, Letter to the Smyrnaeans 8:1; all emphases added.

flesh and blood of that Jesus who was made flesh. For the apostles, in the memoirs composed by them, which are called Gospels, have thus delivered unto us what was enjoined upon them: that Jesus took bread, and when He had given thanks, said, "This do in remembrance of Me" (Luke 22:19), "this is My body"; and that, after the same manner, having taken the cup and given thanks, He said, "This is My Blood"; and gave it to them."[55]

Note: St. Justin Martyr died about A.D. 165. He was the first Christian writer to quote the book of Acts. He also notes above the apostolic memoirs called "Gospels." This was before the Bible's formal codification in the late fourth century. This is **proof** that the Catholic Church practiced the transubstantiation of the Eucharist from the time the apostles handed it down to today.

Let's look at examples of the Eucharist *literally* becoming the Body and Blood of Jesus Himself. Remember, Jesus is divine and human. He is truly present in the Eucharist — and there are more than 150 known eucharistic miracles. A great resource book to use to study many historical Eucharist miracles is *Eucharistic Miracles* by Joan Carroll Cruz. Here are some noteworthy examples of Jesus' Real Presence in the Eucharist for man to see and believe.

The Eucharistic Miracle at Lanciano, Italy

In the year A.D. 750, a priest was celebrating the Holy Sacrifice of the Mass. This priest suffered from recurring doubts regarding transubstantiation, or the Real Presence of Jesus in the Eucharist. Upon speaking the Words of Consecration, the Host was suddenly changed

---

[55] St. Justin Martyr, *First Apology*, in *Ante-Nicene Fathers*, vol. 1, trans. Marcus Dods and George Reith, https://www.newadvent.org/fathers/0126.htm, chap. 66; emphasis added.

into a circle of human flesh and the wine was transformed into visible blood! Upon gaining his composure, he wept and proclaimed to the congregation present in the church, "O fortunate witnesses to whom the Blessed God, to confound my unbelief, has wished to reveal Himself visible to our eyes! Come, brethren, and marvel at our God, so close to us. Behold the Flesh and Blood of our Most Beloved Christ."

The congregation rushed to the altar to see the miracle and word spread as fast as it could in the eighth century. The Flesh remained intact but the Blood in the chalice soon divided into five pellets of unequal size and shape. The Host and the five pellets of Blood were placed in a reliquary. All history records were preserved, and the details of this supernatural miracle are written on parchments in both Greek and Latin.

The ivory reliquary was replaced in 1713 with two relics. The Flesh of Our Lord is preserved in a monstrance the way a eucharistic Host is enclosed. The nuggets of Blood are held in a chalice of etched crystal.

Various authentications have been performed throughout time; however, in 1970, a final verification was performed under strict scientific criteria in an independent study headed by Doctors Odoardo Linoli, a professor of anatomy and pathological histology, and Ruggero Bertelli, a professor emeritus of human anatomy. The report was presented in medical and scientific language on March 4, 1971, to ecclesiastical officials of the Church, civil, judicial, political, and military authorities, medical personnel, and residents. These are the histological results: the flesh was identified as striated muscular tissue of the myocardium heart wall having no agents or materials present that would suggest natural preservation of the human heart tissue.

Both the Flesh and the Blood were determined to be of human origin. The Blood and the Flesh were found to be of the same human blood type, AB. What is truly glorious is that the Blood of the eucharistic miracle was found to also contain the minerals of chlorides, phosphorous, magnesium, potassium, sodium to a lesser degree, and a greater quantity of calcium. Proteins in the Blood were found to be normally fractionated with the same percentage ratio found in **normal fresh blood**.

The AB blood type appears in all eucharistic miracles and is the same blood type on the burial cloth of Jesus, known as the Shroud of Turin, along with the blood type on Veronica's veil, worn by the woman who wiped the blood from Christ's face and brow as He carried His Cross to His death for you and me. This eucharistic miracle is on display in a tabernacle in the Church of St. Francis in Lanciano today.

But eucharistic miracles are not just found in the distant past. In the twenty-first century, there have been four more eucharistic miracles. Let us look at a recent one.

The Eucharistic Miracle at Sokolka, Poland

On October 12, 2008, at St. Anthony's Catholic Church, a consecrated Host accidentally fell to the floor during distribution of the Eucharist. Following Church protocol and to dispose of the consecrated Host properly, it was placed in a vascular to dissolve by the parish sacristan, Sr. Julia Dubowska. The Host began to discolor, and the pastor thought that it was simply dirt from the floor where it fell. The stained Host was placed back in the tabernacle on a small corporal, where it remained for three years. A histological study was done along with independent tests performed. All parties agreed that the Host was human cardiac muscle tissue from the upper left ventricle (as was the case at Lanciano, Italy). The structure of the transformed Host is identical to the myocardial heart tissue of a living person at death. The heart muscle fibers were examined under electron microscope and were found to be inseparably connected at the molecular level with those of the "bread" in a manner that is not humanly or scientifically possible.

The Catholic Church professes that after the Words of Consecration are spoken by the priest, invoking the power of the Holy Spirit, the bread and wine are transformed into the Body and Blood of Christ. We are unaware of any such eucharistic miracles occurring in any other church of man that have been scientifically studied and verified as supernatural.

Supernatural Proof #2: Incorruptibility of Human Beings after Death

Once again, there is a supernatural phenomenon in the Roman Catholic and Eastern Orthodox Churches whereby human bodies defy the natural process of decomposition. We all know that the human body is two-thirds water or liquid. So, how can a body be incorrupt centuries post-death? The answer is that God wills it to be. His divine intervention allows some bodies to not see decay.

There are hundreds of Catholic saints and blesseds whose bodies have not decayed. Although it is not a prerequisite for canonization as a saint in the Catholic Church, many of these people have, in fact, been recognized as saints in the Catholic Church. Incorruptibility gives witness to the truth of the resurrection of the body and the life to come. There are over three hundred people (mostly women) who are purported to be incorruptible. Let us briefly share a few of these holy, pious followers of Christ. These people lived lives of heroic virtue and utmost devotion to God. God has thus preserved them as a reminder of His faithfulness to His elect.

St. Rita of Cascia (1381–1457)

St. Rita the Miracle Worker and Saint of Impossible and Desperate Causes is remarkably incorrupt. At the age of twelve, the young pious girl was given in marriage (against her wishes) by her elderly parents. During eighteen years of marriage, St. Rita and her husband produced two sons. Her husband was violently abusive and often beat his prayerful wife. He was assassinated due to political motives, but before this occurred, her home was at peace due to the transformation caused by her long-suffering and persistent prayers.

After her husband's murder, she was led to more trials and suffering, as her two sons wished to avenge their father's murder. Rita prayed for their hearts to be changed rather than for them to commit murder themselves. Her prayers were once again answered, and both died in union with the Church, forgiving their father's murderers.

St. Rita then applied to enter the convent of the Augustinians in Cascia. However, the rule of the order was not to accept widows. Again, she prayed, and her prayers were answered when her patron saints — Augustine, Nicholas of Tolentino, and John the Baptist — appeared to her one night and accompanied her to the convent. Despite having bolted gates and locked doors, these miraculously opened to allow her to gain access to the chapel. The following morning, the sisters discovered her inside their chapel, and they concluded that the entry into their locked chapel was the will of God. They admitted her to their order.

She longed to suffer as Christ Himself, and she was granted a thorn wound in her forehead which would fester and produce an offensive odor. She spent the next fifteen years of her life in reverential seclusion. Three days before her death at age seventy-six, St. Rita was given a vision of Our Lord and His Holy Mother. At the time of her death in her cell, the room was filled with a perfume smell and bright light emanated from the wound on her forehead.

Many miracles have been attributed to St. Rita's intervention with Jesus. Her body was never properly entombed. Several documented supernatural occurrences have happened to her body over the years: her eyes would open unaided, her body at times would move to one side or the other after years, and the elevation of the entire body to the top of the sarcophagus was also observed by eyewitnesses. Her body can be seen at St. Rita's Basilica in Cascia, Italy.

St. Teresa of Ávila (1515–1582)

St. Teresa of Ávila was a pious child and took her religious vows with the Carmelite Order in Ávila, Spain in 1534. She reformed her order, replacing laxity with rigorous piety and devotion. She was a mystic and frequently communicated with Jesus. She left us three masterful spiritual writings, including her autobiography, *The Way of Perfection*, and *The Interior Castle*, which is considered to be her greatest work. She was never a healthy woman and died on October 4, 1582. The delightful fragrance that enveloped her cell while she was alive emanated from her grave. Her body was exhumed on July 4, 1583. The saint's confessor, Francisco de Ribera, wrote the following to document what they saw:

> The coffin was opened … nine months after interment; the coffin lid was smashed, half rotten and full of mildew … the clothes had fallen to pieces…. The holy body was covered with the earth which penetrated into the coffin and was also damp too, but as fresh and whole as if it had been buried the day before … They undressed her almost entirely for she had been buried in her habit — they washed the earth away, and there spread through the whole house a wonderful penetrating fragrance which lasted days … They put her in a new habit, wrapped her in a sheet and put her back into the same coffin.[56]

[56] Joan Carroll Cruz, *The Incorruptibles*, (Gastonia: TAN Books, 1974), p.187

There is also the story of her heart being pierced. She records this in her autobiography when she describes one of her transverberations, or spiritual ecstasies. She writes, "I saw an angel close by me, on my left side, in bodily form.... He was not large, but small of stature, and most beautiful — his face burning, as if he were one of the highest angels, who seem to be all of fire.... I saw in his hand a long spear of gold, and at the iron's point there seemed to be a little fire. He appeared to me to be thrusting it at times into my heart, and to pierce my very entrails; when he drew it out, he seemed to draw them out also, and to leave me all on fire with a great love of God."[57]

St. Teresa of Ávila's wounded pierced heart was meticulously examined in 1872 by three physicians. They noted the perforations made by the dart. They agreed that the preservation of her heart could be explained by scientific or natural causes. Her body was re-examined in 1914, and it was in the same condition as before with the same flowery fragrance permeating from it. In 1970, St. Teresa of Ávila was named the first woman Doctor of the Church.

St. John of the Cross (1542–1591)

Another Doctor of the Church, St. John of the Cross served as the confessor at the convent in Ávila where St. Teresa was the prioress. St. Teresa wrote of him, "He is one of the most purest souls in the Church of God." The sisters witnessed many of his levitations during ecstatic prayer. He too was a mystic and, despite being persecuted and imprisoned by superiors within the Church, he wrote some of the best mystical theology ever written. His works include *The Ascent of Mt. Carmel*, *The Dark Night of the Soul*, and *The Spiritual Canticle*.

---

[57] St. Teresa of Ávila, *The Life of St. Teresa of Ávila* (New York: Cosimo Classics, 2011), chap. 29, 16–17, pp. 225–226.

He died after a painful illness at age forty-nine and was buried in a vault beneath the floor of a church. On the Monday following the burial, the friars noted a great light emanating from his tomb that lasted for several minutes. His body was exhumed and carefully examined in 1859, 1909, and again in 1955. His body in 1955 was found to be perfectly moist and flexible, like a living human being. His body is in the convent of the Discalced Carmelites of Segovia, Spain, the order that he founded.

Sr. Wilhelmina (1924–2019)

Recently in the United States, Sr. Wilhelmina Lancaster, the prioress and founder of the Benedictines of Mary Queen of Apostles, was exhumed and found to be incorrupt. She died at age ninety-five. She can be viewed in the Abbey of Our Lady of Ephesus Church in Gower, Missouri.

Supernatural Proof #3: The Apparitions of Our Blessed Mother, Mary

The appearances of the Blessed Virgin Mary have occurred consistently over the centuries. She can only appear to mankind with the authority and will of God. These sightings offer further support and encouragement for our spiritual lives. Like the New Eve, she is the Mother of all the living Christians in the New Testament. God Himself allows her to appear on earth and her messages are of critical importance to the peoples of the world. She is constantly pointing humanity back to her Son, Jesus, and seeking more devotion, worship, prayer, and repentance — just like St. John the Baptist and Jesus preached.

There have been many private revelations of visitations by our Blessed Mother. There have been over three hundred of these that have occurred. However, the Church, after scrutiny regarding divine origin, has only approved twenty-six.

Belief in these apparitions is not a formal requirement of the Catholic faithful. But Mary constantly shares that her prayers for us are offered to God for the conversion of souls. She wants nothing more than to lead us to Jesus, Her Son. She is the Mother of the Church and became the first Christian the moment she said yes to God's invitation to incarnate His Word in her womb. She *literally* birthed the Church. Like a faithful, loving Mother, she guides her children into the love of the Father, and in safeguarding salvation, she appears to the Church Militant on earth.

Let us look at a few Church-approved apparitions.

Our Lady of Guadalupe, Mexico

Our Blessed Mother appeared to a peasant, Juan Diego, between December 9 and December 12, 1531. She left a miraculous image on his *tilma* (his outer shawl-like garment made of cactus husks) as proof of her visitation to the bishop, the Church, and the native peoples of modern-day Mexico. Normally, a *tilma* would deteriorate completely after about thirty years. Juan Diego's *tilma* is still in perfect condition.

The image on the *tilma* depicts her as the woman of Revelation 12: the pregnant Jewish Mother about to give birth to Emmanuel. The miraculous *tilma* is on display at the Basilica of Our Lady of Guadalupe in Mexico City. Scientists cannot determine how or why this image is preserved as the *tilma* colors of her image did not exist on the rainbow spectrum and could not be humanly made as pigments in 1531. It has miraculously survived an accidental spilling of nitrous acid upon it in 1795 — and even a failed Communist bombing attempt to destroy the sacred and supernatural *tilma*.

It was November 14, 1921, when at 10:30 a.m., a bomb went off inside the Church directly below the *tilma* housed in a glass case. The bomb had been planted by a Mason at the base of the image, disguised within flowers. The explosion destroyed the sanctuary and violently bent the cast-iron crucifix of Our Risen Lord backward toward the image of Our Lady of Guadalupe on the *tilma*. The explosion was so powerful that the windows of houses outside the church were shattered. But the single-pane glass covering the *tilma* was not even cracked. The *tilma* did not suffer the slightest of damage. Jesus on the Cross *literally* protected His mother from the harm that man wished to cause to her supernatural image.

Mary's appearances at Guadalupe led to the conversion of many Aztecs to Catholicism. The Aztecs had practiced pagan human sacrifice, but after the appearance of Our Blessed Mother, a Christian culture of life replaced a diabolical culture of death.

Her appearance validated three of the four Marian dogmas of the Church. Mary appeared with a material body, confirming her Assumption into Heaven. She called herself "The Mother of God" and "Ever Virgin." Although the name *Guadalupe* is thought to be Spanish in origin, in the local Aztec dialect it sounds remarkably like the words meaning 1) "She who is without stain" and 2) "She who crushes [the] stone serpent."

In the actual image, Mary stands on a dark crescent moon which was the symbol of the Aztec serpent god. Our Lady stepping on the serpent in the image conveys the Immaculate Conception. She is the "woman" referred to in Genesis 3:15 who is at complete enmity with Satan and sin itself. God revealed His Mother, Mary, as the woman of Revelation 12. The Aztec demon-worshiping religion was conquered by God, who allowed His Mother to appear, and evil was overcome. Christianity was planted in the New World. This is factual history, not fiction.

Moreover, this all occurred during the Protestant Reformation in Europe and England. It is estimated that five million Catholics voluntarily or involuntarily (by state mandate) left the Catholic Church (in some places, the state made it very difficult to remain Catholic by threatening confiscation of one's property and goods or imprisonment and possible death) during the initial Reformation period of the sixteenth century. Meanwhile, in the New World of the North American continent, over nine million Aztecs converted to Catholicism during the first nine years after the apparitions. That is an average of 2,900 individuals per day.

Today, the basilica that houses the *tilma* is one of the most visited Christian sites in the world, second only to the Holy Land itself.

Our Lady of Lourdes, France

The apparitions of Lourdes are incredibly well-documented and world-renowned. The eighteen apparitions took place in 1858, when the Virgin Mary appeared to St. Bernadette Soubirous. In the course of the appearances, Bernadette was instructed to dig in the dirt with her hands and a spring of water miraculously appeared. Today, twenty-seven thousand gallons appear daily from this spring. Numerous miraculous healings or recoveries occur there associated with faith and the healing water. They are scientifically inexplicable, and are therefore miraculous.

At Lourdes and during apparition number sixteen, Mary herself stated, "I am the Immaculate Conception," meaning that she was conceived without sin. This dogma of the Church was proclaimed in 1854 by Pope Pius IX in Rome, four years before the apparitions. Bernadette was an illiterate fourteen-year-old peasant girl. When she communicated this message to the local priest, he knew it was of

God, as there was no way that this illiterate young girl would ever know what these words meant.

Through this little girl, God confirmed His Vicar of Christ, the pope. Through this little girl, Mary urged all to pray the Rosary for penance and reparation for the sins of humanity.

As an added note, St. Bernadette died at age thirty-five. She is, to this day, incorrupt and appears to be simply sleeping. Her body can be seen at the chapel of the convent of St. Gildard in Nevers, France.

Our Lady of Fátima, Portugal

Perhaps the most important of all Marian apparitions occurred in Fátima, Portugal, where our Blessed Mother Mary appeared over six consecutive months in 1917. She warned the world of the evils that would afflict the globe in the twentieth century, particularly with major world wars. She assured us that, in the end, her Immaculate Heart would triumph over this age of darkness. To hasten the victory over darkness, she urged conversion, penance, and the daily Rosary along with the five first Saturday devotions. She warned that Communism (atheism) along with its totalitarianism would cause cataclysmic harm to humanity because if it accepts them, it will have abandoned the Christian faith.

God confirmed the message at Fátima by performing the most amazing miracle seen by mankind in modern times. On October 13, 1917, the sun began to zigzag over the sky and then began to plummet toward the earth. Between seventy thousand and one hundred thousand people witnessed this event. They began screaming and panicking, thinking that they were about to die; but before it hit the earth, the sun halted its trajectory, shot back up to the sky, and fixed itself again. The miracle was specifically pre-announced by Mary herself. Many reporters and atheists were there to witness and record this event. It is preserved for human history by photographs, film, and eyewitness accounts. It is a shame that the majority of the world is unaware of these facts.

Supernatural Proof #4: The Raising of the Dead

The Bible records ten incidents of resurrection from mortal death — three in the Old Testament and seven in the New Testament.

In the Old Testament, the first one raised is the son of the widow of Zarephath: Elijah stretches himself over the dead boy and cries out to God and life returns to him (1 Kings 17:8–24). The second is when Elijah's successor, Elisha, raises the Shunammite woman's son from the dead (2 Kings 4:18–37). Finally, an unnamed man whose dead body is thrown on top of Elisha's dead bones also rises from the dead (2 Kings 13:20–21).

In the New Testament, Jesus raises the son of a widow from Nain upon witnessing the boy's grieving mother during his funeral procession (Luke 7:11–17). Jesus also resurrects Jairus's daughter (Mark 5:21–43). The raising of Lazarus by Jesus also is witnessed by many and is very prominent in Scripture as well (John 11). Another spectacular example of the raising of the dead is in Matthew 27:52–53, when Our Lord died on the Cross: "Tombs also were opened, and many bodies of the saints who had fallen asleep were raised, and coming out of the tombs after his resurrection they went into the holy city and appeared to many." This mass resurrection is indicative of Jesus' victory over death, as these many holy ones are seen walking around Jerusalem. (Can you imagine what people would have thought?) Of course, Jesus Himself was resurrected, in the Miracle of miracles. Finally, after Jesus' Resurrection and Ascension, Peter raised Tabitha, or Dorcas, from the dead (Acts 9:36–43), and Paul raised Eutychus from the dead (Acts 20:7–12).

In commissioning the twelve apostles, Jesus gave powers to work miracles to witness to His divine source of power given to them and their teachings. In Matthew 10:8, Jesus commands them, "Heal the sick, **raise the dead**, cleanse lepers, cast out demons. You received without pay, give without pay" (emphasis added). Once again, at the Last Supper, Jesus conveys supernatural powers upon the apostles, as recorded in John 14:11–12: "Believe me that I am in the Father and the Father in me; or else believe me for the sake of the works themselves [miracles]. Truly, truly, I say to you, **he who believes in me will also do the works that I do; and greater works than these will he do**, because I go to the Father" (emphasis added).

There is nothing more important than to know that you will be resurrected from the dead. This is our great hope and the basis of our faith.

Amazingly, since biblical times there have been over four hundred additional, documented resurrections of dead people, performed at the hands of priests and religious within the Church by the power of the Holy Spirit given to them as successors of the apostles. Notable raisings of the dead were performed by St. Hilary of Poitiers, St. Ambrose, St. Martin of Tours (he raised three separate people from the dead), St. Bernard of Clairvaux, St. Anthony of Padua, St. Dominic, St. Ignatius of Loyola, St. Paul of the Cross, St. Philip Neri, St. John Bosco, St. Rose of Lima, St. Martin de Porres, St. Patrick, and St. Vincent Ferrer to name but a few.

A great book to learn the details of the events and circumstances of the resurrections of dead people by the Church is *Raised from the Dead: True Stories of 400 Resurrection Miracles*, by Fr. Albert J. Hebert, S.M.

It is just as Jesus said in Matthew 11:4–5, "**Go and tell John what you hear and see … the dead are raised up**" (all emphases added), or as St. Paul testified to the world in Acts 26:8, "Why is it thought incredible by any of you that God raises the dead?" Again, Scripture records in Acts 9:41–42, "He [Peter] gave her his hand and lifted her up. Then ... he presented her alive.... And many believed in the Lord."

The Supernatural Proves God's Love for Us

The examples given above present four separate topics and diverse proofs of the supernatural activity alive within the Church Jesus Himself established. They all have one common element: God.

"God is love" (1 John 4:16). Therefore, God must be a Trinity of Persons. Why? Because love requires three things: a lover (the Father), a beloved (the Son) and a relationship between them of love that is the Holy Spirit. The Holy Spirit has continued to demonstrate God's love for us by allowing these events to occur within His Church and for the whole world to see.

Christians accept that Jesus rose from the dead, which proves that He came from God and that the Spirit of God, and the power of God, rests upon Him. For Christ Himself testified that He is God. Christians also believe that God is still able to perform miracles. But miracles must be subjected to reason and to scientific, medical, and ecclesiastical analysis by experts to validate that they are not of any known human origin. When miracles such as the ones above that have passed these rigorous tests are denied by people that suspend rational thought and deny empirical evidence by an act of their own free will, they are being intellectually dishonest. However, many Christians and non-Christians repudiate the evidence of the supernatural. Indeed, many non-Catholic Christians deny the supernatural events that have occurred in Jesus' Catholic Church. These dismissals take one of three forms: rejection of the truth (which is like bearing false witness against your neighbor), ignoring the truth (which is a form of intellectual dishonesty), or suggesting that the supernatural is from Satan to deceive people. Remember, it is a sin to attribute to Satan what is the work of the Spirit of Truth.

It is important to pause here and consider Jesus' words. Jesus Christ called the Holy Spirit the "Spirit of truth" (John 14:17; 15:26; 16:13). Jesus also warned all mankind twice about this sin, as it is unforgivable and impacts your salvation. For He said, "Therefore I tell you, every sin and blasphemy will be forgiven men, but the **blasphemy against the Spirit will not be forgiven**. And whoever says a word against the Son of man will be forgiven; **but whoever speaks against the Holy Spirit will not be forgiven, either in this age or the age to come [after death]**" (Matt. 12:31–32; all emphases added). Jesus stated this directly again by saying, "Truly, I say to you, all sins will be forgiven the sons of men, and whatever blasphemies they utter; **but whoever blasphemes against the Holy Spirit never has forgiveness, but is guilty of an eternal sin** — for they had said, 'He has an unclean spirit'" (Mark 3:28–30; emphasis added).

Supernatural miracles should serve as proof that God, through Christ, is showing His divine approval and caring for His true Church founded by Jesus. His Church is the Ark of Eternal Salvation, His one true Bride. For approximately two thousand years, He has continued to demonstrate that His supernatural powers remain in her. These miracles are God's testimony to the truth of the Catholic Church and the Catholic Faith.

Yet many still do not believe. "Now when they heard of the resurrection of the dead, some mocked" (Acts 17:32).

REFLECTIONS

1. Do you think that the church you attend will be in existence in fifty, one hundred, or five hundred years from now?

2. Why do supernatural events only occur in Catholic or Orthodox Churches?

3. Do you know of any non-Catholic Christian that has died and their body is incorrupt?

4. Do you know any non-Catholic Christians who have possessed the stigmata, the wounds of Christ?

Chapter 9

Unity and Continuity Do Matter to God

Our Lord asked "that they may also be in us." (John 17:21)

Christian unity occurs when we participate as one Body in the Life of the Blessed Trinity. The life of grace was bestowed upon us in Baptism, strengthened in Confirmation, and is renewed daily if we receive Christ in the Holy Eucharist and are cleansed of our sins in Confession.

These are but four of the sacraments that His Church has given mankind. And this life of grace is the Life of the Trinity that dwells in our souls.

Our Lord also included in His final prayer the desire "that they may all be one; even as thou, Father, art in me, and I in thee, that they also may be in us, so that the world may believe that thou hast sent me" (John 17:21). True unity is visible, doctrinal, and spiritual. When will Muslims, pagans, Jews, and atheists believe in the Lord Jesus Christ? It seems unlikely to occur until at least all Christians are united under His universal pastor, the pope, and His bishops.

The Catholic Church was not founded by a mere human being; it was founded by God incarnate.

There are only two religions in the history of the world that have been started by God: Old Testament Judaism and New Testament

Catholicism. Judaism is pre-messianic Catholicism and Catholicism is post-messianic Judaism. This is the Kingdom of God timetable: 1) David established 2) Solomon continued 3) Jesus completed. The Church is the extension of the Davidic Kingdom of Christ through Peter. Thus, all seven sacraments of the Catholic Faith are based on Jewish roots.

The Catholic Church is the only Church that has authority given to her by God Himself. No church founded by a mere mortal can show a single Bible verse that gives any person the authority to found another church other than the one founded by Jesus Christ. The Catholic Church's Magisterium is the spiritual government set up by God to teach, govern, and sanctify every man, woman, and child. St. Paul reminds us, "Let every person be subject to the governing authorities. **For there is no authority except from God,** and those that exist have been instituted by God. **Therefore he who resists the authorities resists what God has appointed, and those who resist will incur judgment**" (Rom. 13:1–2; all emphases added).

This book has emphasized that there is only one Church that has the fullness of Truth. Scripture notes Jesus making this promise to His Church: "I have yet many things to say to you, but you cannot bear them now. When the **Spirit of truth comes,** he will guide you **into *all the truth;* for he will not speak on his own authority, but whatever he hears he will speak, and he will declare to you the things that are to come**" (John 16:12–13; all emphases added).

Jesus Christ founded only one Church and entrusted to her the fullness of grace and Truth. Is it intellectually honest to think that the Holy Spirit is teaching something different to thousands of other Christian denominations founded by mere mortals and not by Jesus? As we have shared earlier, St. Paul reinforces St. John's ecclesiology by saying, "If I am delayed, you may know how one ought to behave in the **household of God, which is the church of the living God, the**

pillar and bulwark of the *truth*" (1 Tim. 3:15; emphasis added). Notice in the verse that the word *church* is singular. The Holy Spirit will teach God's one Church the Truth. To reject Christ's Church is to reject God's authority over humankind.

Does God err? Of course not. So why is there disunity? Why are there tens of thousands of U.S. tax code non-defined "churches" in the United States? The answer is basic and simple. Virtually every one of these so-called "churches" teaches something different based on the private interpretation of its founder or pastor. Indeed, most will readily admit that they do this.

What is the problem with plurality of Christian denominations? Schism is a wound to the Body of Christ. American Evangelical Christians are proud of their individualist Christianity. But their faith is about them. They forget that Sacred Scripture and historical tradition are clear that Christians should not stand compartmentalized and apart. They must stand within the larger single Body of Christ. To truly believe in Christ means to desire unity, and to desire unity means to desire the true Church. Even the Holy Bible is part of the tradition (historical practice) of His Church, for He gave it to His true Church, all seventy-three books. To narrow it to sixty-six books post-reform wounds Him dearly.

Protestants like to argue that they are somehow "one" with the Catholic Church as Christians. But let us look at it from a reverse perspective: Why do Catholics believe that their Church is the one true Church of Jesus Christ? Wouldn't it be more reasonable to believe that Christ's true Church is a spiritual union of all Christian denominations? The simple answer is no.

Here are the reasons why Catholics believe that their Church is the one true Church of Jesus Christ: 1) the Catholic Church is the only Christian Church that goes back in human history to Christ Himself; 2) the Catholic Church is the only Christian Church that possesses invincible unity, intrinsic holiness, continual universality, and the indisputable apostolic foundation that Christ said would distinguish His true Church; 3) the apostles and Church Fathers, who certainly were members of Christ's true Church, all professed to be members of this same Catholic Church; and 4) the Catholic Church alone possesses the four marks of *one* united Church, for she is not a collection of competing churches, **holy**, for she is the Bride of Christ, *catholic*, for she is a universal whole Church founded on every continent preaching the **same Gospel message**, and *apostolic*, for she came from Christ through the apostles. The Holy Mass that occurs daily all around the world is the same.

In Acts 11:26, it says, "In Antioch the disciples were for the first time called Christians." St. Evodius was one of the seventy-two chosen by Jesus. He succeeded St. Peter as the bishop of Antioch and died in A.D. 66. It was this bishop that was the first person to use the word *Christian*. Upon his death, his successor was St. Ignatius of Antioch, a disciple of St. John the Evangelist. He was appointed by St. Peter and would govern the Catholic Church in Antioch for over forty years.

Many biblical scholars believe that Ignatius was the child whom Jesus took in his arms and offered to the apostles as an example of humility (Matt. 18:2). St. Ignatius wrote, "Be subject to the bishop and to one another, as Jesus Christ was subject to the Father, and the apostles were subject to Christ and the Father, so that there may be unity,"[58] and "**Where the bishop is present**, there let the congregation gather, **just as where Jesus Christ is, there is the Catholic Church**."[59]

[58] William A. Jurgens, *The Faith of the Early Fathers* vol. I (Collegeville: Liturgical Press the Liturgical Press, 1970), p. 20; Collegeville, Minnesota ; vol 1, William A. Jurgens; p. 20; emphasis added.
[59] William A. Jurgens, *The Faith of the Early Fathers* vol. I (Collegeville: Liturgical Press the Liturgical Press, 1970), p. 20; Collegeville, Minnesota ; vol 1, William A. Jurgens; p. 25; emphasis added.

The words *Catholic Church* utilized by St. Ignatius of Antioch in Greek were *ekklesia katholikos*. *Katholikos* is derived from combining two words, *kata* meaning "concerning" and *holos* meaning "whole." So, it literally means "regarding the whole," or is simplified as "universal." *Ekklesia* means "those called out"; therefore, today's Catholic Church is comprised of those clergy and laity who were called out by Christ to gather into His universal Body.

Our Lord was very clear when saying, "So there shall be **one flock, one shepherd**" (John 10:16; emphasis added). Today, it is well known that the various Protestant and non-denominational sects cannot agree on what Christ taught. They are all practicing disunity. Protestantism and all its accelerating derivations in the twentieth and twenty-first centuries can never unite or be unified. They do not teach nor believe in the same fundamentals, neither of doctrines nor of principles. Yet many profess to be "one." Again, their congregation's "unity" is defined by each separate pastor, as some accept certain churches and not others as Christian. Their own congregational separations go much deeper when you ask the individual Christian member — which Christian churches are real Christians versus which ones are non-Christian? This is the true acid test of their own hypocrisy. The reader should simply give the chart of all the churches in this book and ask a non-Catholic Christian this basic simple question — which churches on this list are Christian and which ones are not Christian? So much for unity amongst the Protestants, yet most profess to be part of Christ's true Church. We rest our case — who is telling the truth when they all claim to be doing so?

Christ emphatically condemned denominationalism when He said, "And if a house is divided against itself, that house will not be able to stand" (Mark 3:25). The Catholic Church teaches that Jesus would never sanction division in His Church.

The Catholic Church also never attacks these other denominations. If you notice, the Church is painfully silent; praying and hoping for these lost sheep to come back into His one flock. However, renouncing one's personal authority for scriptural interpretation is difficult for many because it requires humility. It also requires an act of the human will to admit that I may not be correct in my Christian faith. Still, the true Church patiently waits in hopeful charity.

Here are some examples of what the Catholic Church teaches concerning her proper role in the world as she sojourns to meet her Bridegroom, Jesus Himself. Catholics do not believe that God the Trinity would ever sanction division in His Church. This is simply based on the clear teachings of Sacred Scripture. Unity is necessary and a prerequisite from Christ. Christ said it and the apostles demanded it in their writings. To be in unity and union with Holy Mother Church one must submit to her authority. Christians who maintain the one true Church and practice the one true Faith are Catholic. St. Augustine summarized this well when he addressed heresies and heretics in his time, writing, "Every Catholic Christian is bound to give no credence to these doctrines (other doctrines) … and whoever adheres to any of them, will not be a Catholic Christian."[60]

The *Catechism of the Catholic Church* states, "The duty of offering God genuine worship concerns man both individually and socially. This is 'the traditional Catholic teaching on the moral duties of individuals and societies toward the true religion and the one Church of Christ.'… The social duty of Christians is to respect and awaken in each man the love of the true and the good. It requires them to make the worship of the **one true religion which subsists in the Catholic and apostolic Church**" (CCC 2105, emphasis added).

---

[60] *De Haerisibus*, Epilogue.

From Vatican II, the Decree on Ecumenism: "**Christ the Lord founded one Church and one Church only**. However, many Christian communities present themselves to men as the true inheritors of Jesus Christ; all indeed profess to be followers of the Lord but differ in mind and go their different ways, as if Christ Himself were divided (1 Cor. 1:13). Such division openly contradicts the will of Christ, scandalizes the world, and damages the holy cause of preaching the Gospel to every creature."[61]

The decree goes on to state, "The Church, then is God's only flock."[62]

From Vatican II, the Declaration on Religious Freedom states, "We believe that this **one true religion subsists in the Catholic and Apostolic Church**, to which the Lord Jesus committed the duty of spreading it abroad among all men ... Religious freedom, in turn, which men demand as necessary to fulfill their duty to worship God, has to do with immunity from coercion in civil society. Therefore it leaves untouched traditional Catholic doctrine on the moral duty of men and societies toward **the true religion and toward the one Church of Christ**."[63]

In his encyclical *Mystici Corporis Christi* (June 29, 1943), Pope Pius XII states that "schism, heresy or apostasy" are examples of a sin "such as of its own nature to sever a man from the Body of the Church."[64]

What about unity from the non-Catholic perspective? Could or should all the various sects of Protestantism unite? The answer is

---

[61] Vatican Council II, Decree on Ecumenism *Unitatis redintegratio* (November 21, 1964), no. 1; emphasis added.
[62] Vatican Council II, *Unitatis redintegratio*, no. 2.
[63] Vatican Council II, Declaration on Religious Freedom *Dignitatis humanae* (December 7, 1965), no. 1; all emphases added.
[64] Pius XII, Encyclical Letter on the Mystical Body of Christ *Mystici corporis Christi* (June 29, 1943), no. 23.

that this will never occur. The hallmark of all of them resides in private and personal interpretation of the Bible, various revisions of the Bible, and self-proclamation of new books as somehow "divine" without any substantiated proof (e.g., the Book of Mormon).

But remember, some people's private interpretation and doctrines they derive can even be demonic (see 1 Tim. 4:1). The Bible can be rightly interpreted and wrongly interpreted (see 2 Tim. 2:15). Remember also that even Satan can quote Scripture out of context (see Matt. 4:1–11).

All the churches today (excluding the Catholic Church and Orthodox Church) stem from the Protestant Reformation. All these denominations are called "Protestant" because they only unite on one matter: namely, they all protest their mother, the Catholic Church by rejecting her outright. Today there are tens of thousands of them and they continue to splinter and fragment within themselves because they possess differing interpretations of the Bible, different salvation theories on how one is "saved," and virtually no sacraments from Our Lord.

There is only one Christ and one Pillar of Truth, His Church. There is no Magisterium at all within these churches. So, there is no teaching authority whatsoever. Logic would hold that this method of private interpretation of the Bible is fundamentally wrong: there cannot be one fold, one shepherd, one Faith, and one Baptism when every man and woman distorts and perverts Scripture to suit their own theories.

Protestantism today has fallen into the same error of the ancient Israelites during the period of the Judges: "In those days there was no king in Israel; every man did what was right in his own eyes" (Judg. 21:25). Today we have the King, He is Christ Our Lord. He established His Church on earth as she is in Heaven. She was, is, and ever shall be the Catholic Church, just as Jesus said (see Matt. 16:18).

One of the reasons that the world does not accept Christianity is because of all the division. A person who has never heard of the gospel and discovers all the varieties of Christianity would not believe that Christianity was the Truth, when there is such inconsistency among Christians. They would be totally confused and walk away in the face of such disunity.

The Devil and Disunity

The devil's strategy has always been and will continue to be to divide and conquer us. This started in the Garden of Eden and will continue until Jesus comes again. His *modus operandi* is to separate us from God. Satan is the first liberal. A hallmark of liberalism is to question lawful authority and to become one's own authority. He questioned God's eternal plan for mankind and rebelled against God's authority and His decisions regarding hierarchy. To be very blunt, it is Satan who is the "formal cause" of the divisions and denominations that have occurred within the Body of Christ. Proud human beings are only the "instrumental cause."

The scandal and bad moral behavior of Catholic popes and clergy in the Middle Ages fueled Martin Luther's ire and rebellion. Yes, the facts are clear, he himself rebelled against the authority of Christ's Body, His Church. The Catholic Church acknowledges that *ekklesia semper reformanda est* (the Church must always be reformed); however, true reformation takes place from within the Church, not by breaking off and starting one's own denomination across the street and hurling insults at the true Church.

Fr. Martin Luther would probably have been a saint and not a heretic if he had reformed the Catholic Church from within like other reformer-saints who did precisely that (e.g. St. Thomas More, St. Ignatius of Loyola, St. Philip Neri, St. Charles Borromeo,

St. Teresa of Ávila, St. John of the Cross, St. Francis de Sales), but Luther rebelled instead. True reform comes from within. Scripture is once again clear regarding rebellion: "For rebellion is as the sin of divination, and stubbornness is as iniquity and idolatry" (1 Sam. 15:23) and "An evil man seeks only rebellion" (Prov. 17:11).

God spells out His admonitions clearly in Proverbs 6: "There are six things which the LORD hates, **seven which are an abomination to Him**: haughty eyes, a lying tongue, and hands that shed innocent blood, a heart that devises wicked plans, feet that make haste to run to evil, a false witness who breathes out lies, and **a man who sows discord among brothers**" (vv. 16–19; all emphases added).

The devil had a problem with authority, for out of pride he rebelled against God and still does. Another good example of pride is found in the Old Testament. God chose Moses to lead His people and chose all the sons of Levi for the priesthood to serve the people in the tabernacle. There were Levitical priests named Korah, Dothan, and Abiram along with 250 leaders of the congregation who questioned Moses' authority from God. They rebelled against Moses and God and wanted to separate and be their own congregation. God opened the earth and swallowed up these rebellious men and their entire households. They were sent to Sheol because the Lord despised them for not following Moses, the man He had chosen for His people (cf. Num. 16).

Non-Catholic Christians will push hard against the Catholic Church claiming that she is stained by sin, that she is corrupt, and, for some, that she must be destroyed. But remember, Jesus came to save the sinners, for Scripture recounts, "And as he sat at table in his house, many tax collectors and sinners were sitting with Jesus and his disciples; for there were many who followed him. And the scribes of the Pharisees, when they saw that he was eating with sinners and tax collectors, said to his disciples, 'Why does he eat with tax collectors and sinners?' And when Jesus heard it, he said to them, 'Those who are well have no need of a physician, but those who are sick; I came not to call the righteous, but sinners'" (Mark 2:15–17).

Nonetheless, when the clergy of the Church — those who are supposed to be good shepherds — cause moral scandal, the entire body suffers. Scandals within the Church often deal with sins of the flesh. St. Peter warned the Church when he prophesied about these men within Christ's Church along with their destruction. He said,

> But false prophets also arose among the people, just as there will be false teachers among you, who will secretly bring in destructive heresies, even denying the Master who brought them, bringing upon themselves swift destruction. And **many will follow their licentiousness**, and because of them the way of truth will be reviled.... For if God did not spare the angels when they sinned, but cast them into hell and committed them to pits of nether gloom to be kept until the day of judgment ... then the Lord knows how to rescue the godly from trial, and to keep the unrighteous under punishment until the day of judgment, and especially those who indulge in the lust of defiling passion and **despise authority**. (2 Pet. 2:1–2, 4, 9–10; all emphases added)

So, priests, bishops, cardinals, or the pope himself who defile the grace of ordination by practicing or theologically supporting the LBGTQ lifestyles are in grave danger of eternal punishment. So are clerics who support abortion in any way, shape, or form. These men have great millstones around their necks. They will be held to a high standard by the Lord.

In Jesus' days on earth, the Jews believed that if a person died and their body was lost to the sea and never recovered, then God intended such a person to go to Hell. In other words, it presumed that Hell was this person's eternal destination. This is so important that it is mentioned three times in the Bible. Jesus spoke about this very issue in Matthew 18:6, Mark 9:42, and Luke 17:2. He stated this in the context of causing a little one, or a child, to sin. Jesus states that those who cause them to sin would be better off if they had a millstone hung around their neck and thrown into the sea; implying not only physical death but also that the body would most likely never be recovered. They were doomed.

Did everyone run from the Church of Christ because of Judas? Or did they cease being Catholic because Peter committed the egregious sin of denying Our Lord? No. This is because Catholics are not Catholic because of certain people in the Church. We are Catholic because Jesus Christ established this Church, and we remain loyal to her Head, Christ Himself.

A great exchange was purported to have occurred between Napoleon Bonaparte and a cardinal in Rome. Napoleon stated, "Your Eminence, are you aware that I have the power to destroy the Catholic Church?" The cardinal responded, "Your Majesty, we Catholic clergy have done our best to destroy the Church for the last 1,800 years. We have not succeeded, and neither will you."

There is a great lesson in what Our Lord commanded us about the righteous and the grave sinners coexisting. As we briefly mentioned earlier, the parable of the weeds or tares among the wheat describes well the Catholic Church today. Jesus explains:

> Another parable he put before them, saying, "The kingdom of heaven may be compared to a man who sowed good seed in his field; but while men were sleeping, his enemy came and sowed weeds among the wheat, and

went away. So when the plants came up and bore grain, then the weeds appeared also. And the servants of the householder came and said to him, 'Sir, did you not sow good seed in your field? How then has it weeds?' He said to them, 'An enemy has done this.' The servants said to him, 'Then do you want us to go and gather them?' But he said, 'No; lest in gathering the weeds you root up the wheat along with them. Let both grow together until the harvest; and at harvest time I will tell the reapers, Gather the weeds first and bind them in bundles to be burned, but gather the wheat into my barn.'" (Matt. 13:24–30)

Jesus then explains who the weeds and the wheat are along with all the other references in the parable. Pay particular attention to Our Lord's words:

> Then he left the crowds and went into the house. And his disciples came to him, saying, "Explain to us the parable of the weeds of the field." He answered, "He who sows good seed is the Son of man; the field is the world, and the good seed means the sons of the kingdom; the weeds are the sons of the evil one, and the enemy who sowed them is the devil; the harvest is the close of the age, and the reapers are angels. Just as the weeds are gathered and burned with fire, so will it be at the close of the age. The Son of man will send his angels, and they will gather out of his kingdom all causes of sin and all evildoers, and throw them into the furnace of fire; there men will weep and gnash their teeth. Then the righteous will shine like the sun in the kingdom of their Father. He who has ears, let him hear." (Matt. 13:36–43)

Note the final judgment at the end of time. His angels will harvest all souls, both wheat (good seed) and weeds (bad seed). Those who are weeds will be "gathered out" of Heaven as will "all causes of sin" and "all evildoers." This is a very definitive statement: "all" causes of sin and evildoers. There is no room for error here.

While every Protestant denomination is separated from the Catholic Church, they sometimes make believe that they are spiritually united. But this too is impossible. To have real unity, one must return to the Body of Christ.

St. John the Evangelist was still alive when many popes were already martyred. In the generations following St. Ignatius of Antioch, references to the "Catholic Church" became more and more frequent. St. Polycarp, bishop of Smyrna, who was trained by St. John, on his way to martyrdom prayed for the whole Catholic Church throughout the world. St. Polycarp was burned at the stake around the year A.D. 155. No better name has ever been found to designate the Church Jesus Christ founded than the *Catholic Church*. This was the name she acquired in her earliest years and the name both St. Ignatius of Antioch and St. Polycarp of Smyrna used to define her.

St. Ignatius took for granted that the Catholic Church in Rome had primacy. In his letter to the Romans, he spoke with great respect for the Church in Rome. He writes: "to the church also which holds the presidency in the place of the country of the Romans (1) worthy of God, worthy of honor, worthy of blessing, worthy of praise, worthy of success, worthy of sanctification, and, because you hold the presidency of love, named after Christ and named after the Father: her therefore do I salute in the name of Jesus Christ." St. Ignatius continues in his salutations in his letter to the Philadelphians where he spoke of those who are with "Jesus Christ — they are with the bishop ... there is one bishop with the presbytery and my fellow servants, the deacons." Also, in his letter to the Philadelphians he writes about the threefold ministry of the New Testament when he states: "I spoke with a loud voice, the voice of God: 'Give heed to the bishop and the presbytery and the deacons.'"

There is even an earlier witness to the fact that the Church was indeed apostolic. In approximately A.D. 96, St. Clement of Rome wrote in his Letter to the Corinthians that the apostles of Jesus had "preached in country and city, and appointed their first converts, after testing them by the Spirit, to be bishops and deacons of future believers... They later added a codicil to the effect that, should these die, other approved men should succeed to their ministry."[65]

Based upon these consistent testimonies at the end of the first century and the early second century, there is no doubt that the Church understood herself as apostolic; descending directly from the apostles. History demonstrates that at the end of the first century, there was in place — despite a fairly large geographic area of the ancient world — an organized, visible, institutional, sacerdotal, and hierarchical Church headed in every major city by an ordained leader called a bishop. She was then as she is now: one, holy, catholic, and apostolic Church. She has never ceased to exist nor wavered. Despite her constant persecutions, she remains intact to this very day. Despite the failings of men, some of them leaders of the Church, she is sustained by Jesus' promise of the Paraclete.

Christ was, is, and forever will be constant in purpose. He remains faithful because He cannot deny Himself (2 Tim. 2:13). The Church that He established will remain faithful to Him to the end of the age. This is unity. This is continuity. This is constancy. Remember that His Church is a *Who*. She is His possession belonging to Him, His Mystical Body. His Church is not a *What*; a building or "type" of human-defined church such as a Bible church, a Latter-day

---

[65] William A. Jurgens, *The Faith of the Early Fathers* vol. I (Collegeville: Liturgical Press the Liturgical Press, 1970), p. 20; Collegeville, Minnesota; vol 1, William A. Jurgens; p. 23; emphasis added.

Saint church, or a Baptist church. These are all monikers of man-created churches, for they are "what"-type churches; hence, men named them for what they are — symbolic human precepts. If the Lord is One, then His Church must be one.

"I appeal to you, brethren, by the name of our Lord Jesus Christ, **that all of you agree and that there be no dissensions among you, but that you be united in the same mind and the same judgment**" (1 Cor. 1:10; all emphases added).

Let us close this chapter with some very important questions. Does God err? Of course not. So why do the souls of individual men and women err when it comes to rejecting the Church that Jesus established? Should the mutable substance reject the immutable God? Should he or she who was made by God ignore His Church? These are fundamental questions that we should all prayerfully contemplate. St. Augustine summarized our thoughts when he said "The will of God belongs to the very substance of God.... They [human beings] strive for the savior of eternity, but their mind is still tossed about by past and future movements of things, and is still in vain."[66]

If we abide in Him, we should abide in His Church. Unfortunately, many do not due to their vanity, self-confidence, and in some cases, arrogance. The human mind thinks that it can ascend to the divine. But we didn't create or make ourselves, so what enables a human to think that he or she can create God's Church that has already been created AND ordained by Him?

God, through Christ, established His Church. Human churches can never compare to the one, holy, Catholic, and apostolic Church which is Christ's Bride on earth. The Catholic Church in Heaven is holy and without blemish. This is the Church Triumphant.

---

[66] St. Augustine, *Confessions*, ed. F.J. Sheed, 2nd ed. (New York: Hackett, 2006), p. 240.

REFLECTIONS

1. What is the cause of all division among professed Christians?

2. Why do the historical Protestant sects keep splintering and defecting toward stand-alone, independent churches in the United States?

3. Does your church recognize the teaching authority that Christ gave to His Catholic Church? If not, why?

Chapter 10

Words of Encouragement

*I [Jesus Christ] am the way, and the truth,
and the [eternal] life; no one comes to the
Father, but by me.... If you love me, you will
keep my commandments. (John 14:6, 15)*

We started this book with the last part of the above Scripture quote from Jesus. It is worth reiterating. In the above Scripture, Christ demanded that the apostles keep all His commandments. Since He is the only Way and the only Truth, a human creature should obey all that He taught and commanded us to do. This is obedience to God and His authority. After making this direct statement to the apostles, He promised them that God, through His intercession, would send them the Spirit who would guide them in *all* Truth; thus, we have *one* God, and all three Persons of this triune God stating that Truth would be sent to them. They in turn would build the Church. This is the Catholic Church. Meanwhile, until He comes again, there is a great spiritual battle playing out for the souls of men and women. Most people are inattentive to this great battle. It is real, and one's eternal destiny is at stake.

This book has presented historical facts. But it can also be looked as a "Weapon of Mass Instruction." We have written to you in the light of Christ so that intellectually honest people can understand what has occurred by man playing god. We hope that it will inspire you in Spirit with the love of Christ to come to the knowledge of *who* His Church is. His Body throughout human time is who He represents as His flock.

For you see, brothers and sisters, God took on human nature to save us. God did this because He wants you and loves you, for He created you. He deserves and expects our love of Him and our obedience to His authority which He alone establishes and sustains. He established His Church which is His Mystical Body, or His Bride, until He comes again. Then He will join her as the New Jerusalem, His Bride, the wife of the Lamb (see Rev. 21). He is the Head of His Church. She is the Roman Catholic Church. The foundation of the New Jerusalem, His Mystical Body, are the apostles. Those within the Catholic Church are parts of His Body.

God truly wishes unity for His Body. Satan wishes division and separation. People today are not properly catechized regarding what the Catholic Church teaches relative to salvation nor who she purports to be and why.

We highly recommend reading the *Catechism of the Catholic Church,* 811–870. These sections are concise and clear about who will be saved and why the Catholic Church states this.

What precludes people from learning and growing in their faith and exploring who the Catholic Church says she is? Voluntary ignorance. People chose to not become educated on their own and form their conclusions regarding Truth.

Over the past five hundred years, there has been such strong anti-Catholic rhetoric in the world caused by demonic forces who attack the people of His Church: the leadership, clergy, and the laity. As we have demonstrably noted, it always begins with getting people to reject Church authority which, in turn, yields ignoring her authority given to her by Jesus Himself. The motive to reject her authority lies in the intellect, where one's thoughts exist. Often, people are told falsehoods about the Church, or they use an example of an unholy priest and conclude that the entire Body is bad. Yet the actual action to reject her lies in the person's will. This is where the person acts to formally dissent from not only her authority but also her teachings. In other words, it is normal to "think" or have an intellectual thought that questions the spiritual authority of the Catholic Church. But it is the act of one's will that moves the thought to definitive action. In this action, separation occurs from the Body of Christ. In the person's free will, they choose to reject Jesus' Church.

This rejection and then rebellion against God's Church is exactly what Satan wishes. He too rejected God's authority. Once he made this decision and acted upon it in his will, he rebelled and does so to this very day. Even Satan knows who the true Church is. Consider the black mass celebrated by Satanists: Satanists steal a consecrated Eucharist and desecrate it. Satanists do not steal "communion" wafers from other churches! If God commanded that we follow all His commandments and these include being part of His one, holy, apostolic Church — then we should choose to obey Him.

The Sacraments and the Criticality of Holy Orders

It is worth mentioning the seven sacraments of the Catholic Church, which are: Baptism, Confirmation, Eucharist, Penance, Anointing of the Sick, Holy Orders, and Matrimony. All are given to us for our salvation.

It is important to note that one of the sacraments is that of Holy Orders, the ordination of priests in the Catholic Church. Recall how Jesus gave the apostles His authority to heal the sick, drive out demons, raise the dead, forgive sins, and spread the gospel throughout the ages to all creation. This hasn't ended with the apostles. It continues to this day through the continuous succession of the line of bishops. Many non-Catholics believe that we are all priests and that there is no need for ordained priesthood. Yes, we are all common priests, but Catholicism is rooted in Judaism and what God ordained in the Old Testament continues in the New Testament relative to the ordained priesthood.

The following chart depicts how the Old Testament High Priest is fulfilled by the New Testament High Priest, Jesus Christ. In the Old Testament, we have both the ordained ministerial priests and the common priesthood shared by all Jews. Likewise, in the New Testament, this is fulfilled by the Catholic ordained ministerial priests along with the common priesthood of all Catholic laity. Also, note in the chart the reference to Scripture to support these facts. Ordained priests or ordained deacons primarily administer the sacraments to the laity.

Old Testament:

The High Priest
(cf. Lev 21:10; Matt 26:57)

type of sacrifice offered:
the chief priest was designated to enter the Holy of Holies and perform the religious rites on the annual Day of Atonement (cf. Lev 16)

Ordained, Full-Time Ministerial Priests
(Pre-Levitical – cf. Exod 19:21-22, Levitical – cf. Exod 29ff)

type of sacrifice offered:
animal (cf. Exod 29:10ff), drink (cf. Num 15:10), grain (cf. Lev 2:14ff), etc.

The Common Priesthood Shared by All Jews
(cf. Exod 19:6)

type of sacrifice offered:
spiritual sacrifices to God (cf. Hosea 14:2); also commissioned ordained full-time ministerial priests to offer ritual sacrifice to God on their behalf in the Temple (cf. 2 Macc 12:43).

New Testament:

Jesus Christ
(our "eternal High Priest"
- cf. Heb 7:1-3)

type of sacrifice offered:
His Body & Blood on the cross for the atonement of the sins of humanity
(cf. Luke 23:46)

Ordained, Full-Time Ministerial Priests
(cf. Luke 22:7-20; Rom 15:15-16)

type of sacrifice offered:
all of the sacrifices offered by the members of the common priesthood of all Christians plus the Holy Sacrifice of the Mass – which makes available to individual Christian souls, throughout the course of history, the merits of the once-for-all Sacrifice of Jesus Christ on Calvary (cf. 1 Cor 10:16; 1 Cor 11:23-30)

The Common Priesthood Shared by All Christians
(cf. 1 Pet 2:5; Rev 1:6)

type of sacrifice offered:
spiritual (cf. 1 Pet 2:5), bodies (cf. Rom 12:1), donations (cf. Phil 4:18), praise, good deeds, generosity (cf. Heb 13:15-16); also commissioned ordained full-time ministerial Christian priests to offer the Sacrifice of the Mass to God for their needs and intentions.

Never has there been a time in human history where information is so readily available, yet there exists so much ignorance regarding the Church that Jesus started. But there is nothing new under the sun: St. Thomas More stated, "One of the greatest problems of our time is that many are schooled but few are educated."

Look around and observe how society views the Catholic Church, especially in the United States and Europe. It is hard to be Catholic. It is much easier to dissent and run to a feel-good church; one that is emotionally driven with praise and worship concert-type entertainment with a little Bible reading thrown in. Our culture of death mocks the Church; the media assaults her. Even "cafeteria" Catholics (Catholics in name only) undermine her from within.

Nonetheless, Holy Mother Church was founded by Jesus. As we have shared, the prophet Daniel stated that God would establish His Kingdom in the days of the fourth kingdom: the Roman Empire by a rock that was hewn not of human hands and that would become the messianic kingdom of the world. All future sovereignty would be given to Christ, this Rock. All kingdoms on earth would end and He shall rule over all the nations forever.

Christ knew that He was born to die for the sins of humanity and to conquer death by His immolation. Hence, God chose Peter, Christ named him "Rock" and sent him to Rome where he would be martyred for Christ. Peter had his failings and shortcomings just like Abraham, Moses, and David. This doesn't nullify the fact that Peter was God's chosen one for His Church. However, Jesus promised that the gates of Hell would not prevail against the Church He established by choosing Peter as its human leader. These gates of Hell have not prevailed throughout human history and they will not ever prevail against her.

Again, let's study history. Although the Church has been denigrated and attacked since her conception by Jesus, she has prevailed against Caesar, against heretics, against the Gestapo. Stalin scoffed at her when he said, "How many divisions does the pope have?" But the pope routed Stalin's heirs — astounding but true — and no material weapons were used; only spiritual.

Remember that it is a spiritual battle, and we exhort the reader to start thinking as such. Materialists sometimes point to the fall of the Berlin Wall as marking the fall of communism in 1989. But it actually began in 1979. Between June 2 to 10, 1979, St. John Paul II visited his native Poland. His country had been ruled by the oppressive regime of the Soviet Union. He was warned not to interfere with Poland by the Communist regime. After his visit, millions of Poles formed the Solidarity movement. Their members were virtually all Catholic. This is a great example of the spiritual battle fought without flesh and blood but through the acts of charity within her Church. Yet the Catholic Church was given no credit. In the media we fed the masses that it was U.S. policies, economic sanctions, global political pressure, and our superior weapons that caused the fall of the Berlin Wall. But the credit truly lies with the Catholic Church.

The pope's visit in 1979 would ultimately bring about the collapse of communism in Europe. The Communists would attempt to assassinate him on May 13, 1981, in Rome — the feast day of the appearance of Our Lady of Fátima. But the Church will continue to overcome all dissenters and all zeitgeist that attempt to destroy her. She is the Bride of Christ for all time, for only she has received the eternal promise from God.

Any sensible Christian wants to get closer in relationship with Jesus — and so sensible Christians should get closer to the Catholic Church, as it is His Church, and He reigns from every tabernacle. Only in the Catholic or Orthodox Church is Jesus truly present in the Eucharist. The eucharistic miracles are evidentiary proof. We would encourage readers to come and witness a Mass and ask questions. Everything that you see and hear has profound meaning.

To believe in a church that was not created by Him means that you believe that God and/or Christ erred in some fashion or that God somehow lied and did not send His Spirit to ensure that all Truth was given to His Church. Alternatively, to believe in a church other than the one that God Himself created upon Christ means that a person believes in a church that God somehow "intended in one's mind" from the beginning of time. These suppositions are unsupported propositions, as Scripture itself never proposes or suggests such thinking anywhere. One of the main reasons that our triune God gave His Church universal authority over all spiritual matters through imbuing her with all Truth is so she could be a defense against all human heresies throughout time caused by mankind.

Those who attack, criticize, or vilify the Catholic Church should first discern who she really is — Jesus Christ, Our Lord and Savior. Saul too initially attacked, persecuted, and tried to destroy Christ's Church. As previously mentioned, Scripture records Jesus' own words to a person who attempted to do this, "Why do you persecute *me*" (emphasis added)? **And this person would become St. Paul.** What Jesus said to him in Acts 9:4–5 is self evident: The Catholic Church is *who I AM*.

As human history has shown, men constantly rebel against God and the authoritative structures He establishes. But it was God who revealed Himself to Abraham, Noah, Moses, Simon Peter, the apostles, and Paul. This is divine revelation. From these events, He established a Church for us to worship Him in Spirit and Truth.

Unfortunately, many men and women have defected from Christ's Church. This doesn't change the fact that the Catholic Church is the original Christian Church. She has nourished many of the institutions and disciplines that we take for granted today, from formalized educational systems, healthcare infrastructure such as hospitals, scientific discoveries, legal systems, architecture, farming techniques, art, and music, to name but a few. She has acted heroically and cowardly but despite any human failings, the Church will remain the Bride of Christ and she will be standing at the end of time when Jesus returns. She alone has been given the gifts of infallibility, indefectibility, and indestructibility. She has endured many heresies and will continue to do so. She has flourished despite the Protestant Reformation. She has endured schisms as she awaits her Bridegroom from the days of Peter until today. She began her labors in Rome to spread the good news to all nations and throughout the world. From Europe she would launch Catholic Christopher Columbus, who discovered America even before Protestantism was birthed. She has seen nations and kingdoms rise and fall. She is not a political institution, nor does she seek control over people. She is the spiritual Body of Christ, and thus her body will grow until God the Father sends her Bridegroom, Jesus, to bring her to the Heavenly Kingdom. In the interim, she will continue to see nations and kingdoms rise and fall, and she will still remain.

There will always be only One Lord, One Faith, and One Church. For it is what He commanded.

REFLECTIONS

1. Did God through Jesus create what is today called the Roman Catholic Church?

2. Is His Church the Bride of Christ in Revelation 21?

3. Do you honestly believe that God commanded and intended the creation of thousands of differing churches?

Epilogue

LET US CONCLUDE WITH a prayer.

> *O God, in Thy mercy pour out Thy grace upon those who have gone astray and save those whom Thou hast gathered in Thy Holy Catholic Church. We beseech Thee to pour upon all Christian people the grace of union with Thee and Thy Church, so that putting aside disunion and attaching themselves to the true Shepherd of the Church, they may be able to serve Thee humbly and lovingly, through Christ Our Lord. Amen.*

We encourage everyone to study the Church Fathers and what they wrote and taught. In addition, we encourage you to learn about the heresies that have challenged the Church and read how she dealt with false teachers in their calumny. Finally, as you study your Bible read the Bible with the heart of the Church. The Bible is the great heirloom of the Catholic Church.

Jesus Christ established one Church on earth. To reject the Church that He created for the salvation of mankind is to reject Christ. Pope St. John Paul II in his 1995 writing *Ut Unum Sint* ("That They May Be One") was very clear about unity and the Church. He succinctly said: "To believe in Christ means to desire unity; to desire unity means to desire the Church."[67] We pray that this unity comes to mankind prior to Our Lord's Second Coming.

Some may say, "But I know Him and worship Him." That is good—praise God. But without the Eucharist, there is no eternal life (see John 6:51–59).

St. Paul in his writing to the Ephesians wrote a prayer for the readers of his letter. It is a fitting conclusion to this book.

"Now to him who by the power at work within us is able to do far more abundantly than all that we ask or think, **to him be glory in the church and in Christ Jesus to all generations, for ever and ever. Amen**" (Eph. 3:20–21; emphasis added).

The Catholic Church will provide glory to Christ to all generations forever. Amen.

---

[67] John Paul II, Encyclical Letter on Commitment to Ecumenism *Ut unum sint* (May 25, 1995), no. 9.

About the Authors

JESSE ROMERO IS A full time bilingual Catholic lay evangelist who is nationally recognized for his dynamic Christ-centered preaching. He is a retired Los Angeles deputy sheriff, three-time world police boxing champion and a two-time USA kickboxing champion. Jesse makes the sometimes complex teachings of the Faith understandable with his straight-talk approach. He has a degree from Mount St. Mary's College in Los Angeles and an M.A. in Catholic theology from Franciscan University in Ohio. Recipient of the Archbishop Fulton Sheen Award in 2010 and the Defender of the Faith Award in 2014, Jesse was inducted into the Catholic Sports Hall of Fame in 2015. He hosts two radio podcasts daily on Virgin Most Powerful Radio.

PAUL ZUCARELLI WAS A successful businessman who died unexpectedly on Pentecost 2017. Through the faith of his family and intercessory prayer with Bishop Thomas Olmsted of Phoenix, Paul received a miraculous healing that defies medical science. During his near-death experience, he was given a private revelation of the presence of God and went on to become a nationally recognized Catholic speaker and evangelist. Along with his wife, Beth, Paul bears witness to the power of intercessory prayer, the divine mercy of our Lord, and the love of God to thousands of people. Their apostolate is Faithunderstood.org.

Sophia Institute

Sophia Institute is a nonprofit institution that seeks to nurture the spiritual, moral, and cultural life of souls and to spread the gospel of Christ in conformity with the authentic teachings of the Roman Catholic Church.

Sophia Institute Press fulfills this mission by offering translations, reprints, and new publications that afford readers a rich source of the enduring wisdom of mankind.

Sophia Institute also operates the popular online resource CatholicExchange.com. *Catholic Exchange* provides world news from a Catholic perspective as well as daily devotionals and articles that will help readers to grow in holiness and live a life consistent with the teachings of the Church.

In 2013, Sophia Institute launched Sophia Institute for Teachers to renew and rebuild Catholic culture through service to Catholic education. With the goal of nurturing the spiritual, moral, and cultural life of souls, and an abiding respect for the role and work of teachers, we strive to provide materials and programs that are at once enlightening to the mind and ennobling to the heart; faithful and complete, as well as useful and practical.

Sophia Institute gratefully recognizes the Solidarity Association for preserving and encouraging the growth of our apostolate over the course of many years. Without their generous and timely support, this book would not be in your hands.

www.SophiaInstitute.com
www.CatholicExchange.com
www.SophiaInstituteforTeachers.org

Sophia Institute Press is a registered trademark of Sophia Institute.
Sophia Institute is a tax-exempt institution as defined by the
Internal Revenue Code, Section 501(c)(3). Tax ID 22-2548708.